2013

A BRAND-N...
A PROMIS...

With expert readin... ...can chart a
course to romance... ...n, or career opportunities whil... ...ight into yourself
and others. Offer... ...for 18 full months,
this fascinating guid...

- The important dates in your life
- What to expect from an astrological reading
- How the stars can help you stay healthy and fit
  And more!

Let this sound advice guide you through a year of heav-
enly possibilities—for today and for every day of 2013!

SYDNEY OMARR'S® DAY-BY-DAY
ASTROLOGICAL GUIDE FOR

ARIES—March 21–April 19
TAURUS—April 20–May 20
GEMINI—May 21–June 20
CANCER—June 21–July 22
LEO—July 23–August 22
VIRGO—August 23–September 22
LIBRA—September 23–October 22
SCORPIO—October 23–November 21
SAGITTARIUS—November 22–December 21
CAPRICORN—December 22–January 19
AQUARIUS—January 20–February 18
PISCES—February 19–March 20

IN 2013

SYDNEY OMARR'S®

DAY-BY-DAY ASTROLOGICAL GUIDE FOR

CANCER

JUNE 21–JULY 22

2013

by Trish MacGregor
with Rob MacGregor

A SIGNET BOOK

SIGNET
Published by New American Library, a division of
Penguin Group (USA) Inc., 375 Hudson Street,
New York, New York 10014, USA
Penguin Group (Canada), 90 Eglinton Avenue East, Suite 700, Toronto,
Ontario M4P 2Y3, Canada (a division of Pearson Penguin Canada Inc.)
Penguin Books Ltd., 80 Strand, London WC2R 0RL, England
Penguin Ireland, 25 St. Stephen's Green, Dublin 2,
Ireland (a division of Penguin Books Ltd.)
Penguin Group (Australia), 250 Camberwell Road, Camberwell, Victoria 3124,
Australia (a division of Pearson Australia Group Pty. Ltd.)
Penguin Books India Pvt. Ltd., 11 Community Centre, Panchsheel Park,
New Delhi - 110 017, India
Penguin Group (NZ), 67 Apollo Drive, Rosedale, Auckland 0632,
New Zealand (a division of Pearson New Zealand Ltd.)
Penguin Books (South Africa) (Pty.) Ltd., 24 Sturdee Avenue,
Rosebank, Johannesburg 2196, South Africa

Penguin Books Ltd., Registered Offices:
80 Strand, London WC2R 0RL, England

First Printing, June 2012
10   9   8   7   6   5   4   3   2   1

First published by Signet, an imprint of New American Library,
a division of Penguin Group (USA) Inc.

 REGISTERED TRADEMARK—MARCA REGISTRADA

Printed in the United States of America

PUBLISHER'S NOTE
While the author has made every effort to provide accurate telephone numbers and Internet addresses at the time of publication, neither the publisher nor the author assumes any responsibility for errors, or for changes that occur after publication. Further, publisher does not have any control over and does not assume any responsibility for author or third-party Web sites or their content.

ALWAYS LEARNING   **PEARSON**

CONTENTS

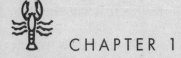

CHAPTER 1

Transformation

We branded 2012 the year of the paradigm shift. And since the world didn't end, here we are at the doorstep of 2013, a year of transformation.

The dictionary meaning of the word is straightforward: a change in form, appearance, nature, or character. Astrologically, this kind of change occurs with the slower-moving outer planets—Pluto, Neptune, and Uranus. They exert the greatest influence over our daily lives because they take so long to move through a single sign. Pluto, for instance, entered Capricorn in 2008 and won't leave until early 2024. Neptune, which takes about fourteen years to move through a sign, entered Pisces in early February 2012 and will be there until late January 2026. Uranus entered Aries in March 2011 and leaves that sign in March 2019. So just these three planets extend a powerful influence over a number of years.

The next two planets that influence us over a period of time are Saturn, which takes two and a half years to transit a sign, and Jupiter, which usually takes about a year. Each of these planets is covered extensively in various parts of the book, and each one has its role in the transformation that will prevail in 2013.

In the next chapter we talk about what each of the planets represents, what signs they rule, and just about anything else you could ever want to know about them astrologically. In a later chapter historical perspectives are provided on the three slowest-moving planets. But this chapter, let's take an in-depth look at the planet Uranus and how its energies will help us through this transformation.

Uranus

This planet symbolizes revolution, genius, rebellion, earthquakes, sudden, unexpected events and change, our individuality, inventions and discoveries, electricity, radio, TV, electronics, lightning. You get the idea. Its energy isn't the least bit subtle. It sweeps into our lives, stirs up mass movements, knocks down the old to make way for the new.

It takes eighty-four years for this planet to move through the zodiac. So let's take a trip down memory lane, to the last time Uranus transited the sign of Aries, the warrior. In mid-January 1928 Uranus entered Aries and remained there until late March 1935. Here are some of the events that occurred during this period:

- First air-conditioned office opens in the U.S. in San Antonio
- Scotch tape first marketed by 3M company
- First trans-Atlantic TV image received

- Amelia Earhart first woman to fly the Atlantic—as a passenger
- Alexander Fleming discovers penicillin
- Yo-yo introduced
- First regularly scheduled TV is broadcast three nights a week
- German airship *Graf Zeppelin* begins a round-the-world flight
- Stock market crash
- Salvador Dali's first one-man show
- Bingo invented
- Planet Pluto named
- Hostess Twinkies invented
- N.Y. Yankee Babe Ruth hits three consecutive homers
- First nudist colony open
- First radar detection of planes
- N.Y. *World* reports disappearance of Supreme Court justice Joseph Crater
- N.Y.C college offers first course in radio advertising
- A bloodless coup d'état in Brazil
- First *Dracula* movie released
- Empire State Building opens in N.Y.C.
- Al Capone is indicted on 5,000 counts of prohibition and perjury
- Babe Ruth hits his 600th home run
- Alka Seltzer goes on sale
- Jane Addams first U.S. woman named corecipient of Nobel Peace Prize
- Martial law is declared in Honduras to stop revolt by banana workers fired by United Fruit
- El Salvador army kills 4,000 protesting farmers

- First patent issued for a tree, to James Markham for a peach tree
- Amelia Earhart is first woman to fly solo across the Atlantic
- Yellow fever vaccine for humans announced
- U.S. federal gas tax enacted
- Earthquake kills 70,000 in Kansu, China
- Hitler proclaims end of Marxism
- Bank holidays declared in six states to prevent run on banks
- FDR inaugurated as thirty-second president, pledges to pull U.S. out of Depression, and says "We have nothing to fear but fear itself."
- FDR proclaims ten-day bank holiday
- Dachau, first concentration camp, completed
- First flight over Mount Everest
- Nazis stage public book burnings in Germany
- Loch Ness Monster is first reported
- German Secret State Police (Gestapo) established
- In London 500,000 march against anti-Semitism
- Alcatraz officially becomes a federal prison
- *Flash Gordon* comic strip debuts
- FDR signs Home Owners Loan Act
- First Sugar Bowl and first Orange Bowl
- First canned beer is sold
- Monopoly is invented
- First Penguin book is published
- 400,000 demonstrators march against fascism in Madrid
- *Billboard* magazine publishes its first music hit parade
- The first stock car race is held in Daytona Beach, Florida

- *Gone With the Wind* by Margaret Mitchell is published
- Spanish Civil War begins, General Francisco Franco leads uprising
- King Edward VIII abdicates throne to marry Mrs. Wallis Simpson

This list represents just a small sampling of the thousands of events that occurred during Uranus' last transit of Aries. But as you read through this list, you undoubtedly see a pattern, right? War, rebellion, uprisings, numerous discoveries and many "firsts," the rise of Hitler and Nazi Germany, natural disasters such as earthquakes, the completion of engineering marvels like the Empire State Building and Hoover Dam, the precipitous drop of the stock market and the Depression that followed.

Aries is not only the sign of the warrior, but of the entrepreneur, the trailblazer, the one who is so independent and forward thinking that he marches to a different drummer. Aries is fearless, a risk-taker, and like the *Star Trek* motto goes where no man (or woman) has gone before. So when you combine Aries with the planet that symbolizes all the traits mentioned earlier, you have an intriguing MO for transformation and tools for navigating it.

There are two facets for this transformation—planetary and personal. Let's start with the planetary.

Planetary Transformation

If the past holds clues about the kinds of events we might expect during this transit, then let's look at the broad patterns:

Medical breakthroughs. During Uranus' last transit of Aries, the medical breakthroughs were significant: treatment for yellow fever, development of penicillin, anesthesia, insulin shock therapy, vitamin B3, and protonsil, the first sulphur drug, which was used to treat infections caused by streptococcus. So this time around we can expect other types of breakthroughs in medicine, health, pharmacology. A cure for AIDS? Cancer? Heart disease?

Rebellion/revolution. The financial meltdown of 2008, the collapse of the housing market, the shakeout in the job market, the election of the first African-American president: the repercussions of these events are still being felt in early 2013 and are likely to echo for some time. The mix of events has given rise to the Tea Party, racism against Muslims and illegal immigrants, religious intolerance.

The "us versus them" mentality has brought about a wider gap between rich and poor, with the middle class fading rapidly. Groups of urban survivalists have sprung up, some of them extremists. The U.S., with the most powerful military in the world (which also eats up the largest chunk of the federal budget), continues to police the rest of the planet, while pushing the needs of its own citizens into a dark hole labeled *later*.

The contentiousness of the political divide in the U.S. was glaringly obvious in the health-care debate that raged for months. Even though a bill was eventually passed, the right kept on screaming about death panels and the left screamed the bill wasn't comprehensive enough. Meanwhile the cost of health care in the U.S. continues to escalate. These trends, unfortunately, may get worse before Uranus leaves Aries.

However, if we remember that Uranus' job is to shake up the status quo so that new paradigms, new ways of doing things, can be born, then we could see the birth of new political parties that emphasize peace over war. Perhaps we'll see a complete withdrawal of U.S. troops from the Mideast or more demonstrations against war.

New social programs. The meltdown in 2008 resulted in massive bailouts to banks, the collapse of institutions, and billions of stimulus dollars poured into the economy. It was the Obama administration's equivalent of FDR's New Deal, passed during his first term in response to the Great Depression. During this period Social Security was implemented.

As Uranus continues its transit through Aries, we may see the implementation of new social programs—such as universal health care mentioned above—or new economic programs that aid people rather than banks and corporations.

Discoveries. Numerous discoveries and inventions came about during Uranus' last pass through Aries. This transit could produce the twenty-first-century equivalents in technology, television, the Internet, health and medicine, engineering, movies, earthquake detection, music, ebooks, alternative fuels.

World records. During Uranus' last transit of Aries many "firsts" occurred, and world records were set.

This time around we could see more of the same—in space flight, cars that run on alternative fuels, high-speed trains, athletics, even the ways our homes and office buildings are powered. The world may go green more quickly than we can imagine.

With Uranus we either embrace change—or it's forced upon us. So let's take a look at how each of us can embrace the change Uranus promises to usher in.

Aries ♈
Cardinal fire sign

As the go-getter of the zodiac, you're probably enjoying Uranus' transit through your sign. It brings all the excitement and adrenaline-powered events that make you feel *alive*.

That said, you generally aren't fond of sudden, un-expected change unless you initiate it. If no area of your life has gone stale or become an empty ritual, then Uranus won't be thrusting anything on you, Aries. You can simply enjoy the wild ride. But if your job, relationships, or career are on remote control, then this transit could be quite a shock, with an abundance of unexpected upsets and changes. Where do you fall in the scheme of things? Uranus has been in Aries for about two years now, so you should have a fairly clear idea how the transit is affecting you.

The best way for you to navigate this transit is to do what you do naturally: maintain a sense of adventure about life; be passionate in all that you undertake; keep your steady focus, don't hesitate to explore. In addition, treat others the way you like to be treated.

In love relationships, strive to be more cooperative, to see things the way your partner does. In your career, with your creative work, complete what you start.

Unusual ideas and idiosyncratic individuals are part of this transit package. You won't be bored, but be careful that life doesn't become just one adrenaline high after the other. Welcome change, embrace it, even if it's thrust on you.

Taurus ♉

Fixed earth sign

You're the most stubborn, resilient, and resolute sign in the zodiac. It's why Taurus is symbolized by the bull! As a fixed earth sign, you like things in your life to be orderly, practical, even predictable. You're slow to change your opinions and beliefs. Stability is your middle name.

The Uranus transit is occurring in your solar twelfth house—your personal unconscious, the most hidden part of your chart. It means that Uranus shakes up your world from the inside out. Issues you have buried, power you have disowned, dreams you've forgotten—all of it surfaces during this transit. Your greatest strength during this period is to tackle one issue at a time and deal with it the way you do everything else in your life—carefully, thoroughly, meticulously. Your dreams should be especially vivid during this transit, and it's to your advantage to remember them, work with them. They contain insights and information that are important.

Unusual people should enter your life during this

transit. Some are teachers, others are students; all will play vital roles. They may disappear as suddenly and inexplicably as they appear.

Gemini ♊

Mutable air sign

Your greatest strengths are your flexibility and communication ability. Both qualities will be enhanced during the Uranus transit through Aries, which forms a beneficial angle to your sun. This transit may not be all bells and whistles; it's a bit more subtle than that. But it brings excitement, change, and unusual people and experiences.

It occurs in your solar eleventh house of friends, wishes, and dreams. More group participation is likely—in theater, writing, bridge, esoterica. Whatever your interests and passions, you find a group of like-minded individuals who share them. In some way they help you to achieve your wishes and dreams.

New opportunities should surface for self-expression. If you've always had a secret yearning to write a novel or screenplay, for example, then this transit helps you to do it. If you're an amateur photographer, you may have an opportunity to become a professional. The transit will free you from limiting circumstances—a relationship that no longer works, a job that has grown stale and predictable, a career that no longer feels right. Your comfortable ruts will become history.

Cancer ♋

Cardinal water sign

The lens through which you see the world is personal, subjective, emotional. Your nurturing and intuitive abilities are your greatest strengths and will serve you well during this transit. Let's take a closer look.

This transit falls in your solar tenth house—career, public persona—and forms a challenging angle to your sun. Abrupt, unexpected changes may challenge your chosen professional course. Your job, for example, could be outsourced. Or you get a new boss whom you don't like. Or you have to take a cut in pay. Whatever the curve ball that Uranus in Aries throws your way, Cancer, you should strive to see it as an opportunity. When the transit is over, you will look back and realize it was exactly that.

When the rug is pulled out from under you, you're forced to use your greatest strengths to forge a new path, a new way of being. So don't hesitate to draw on your intuition during this transit. Seek out the new, the different. Embrace change.

Leo ♌

Fixed fire sign

The transit of Uranus through Aries should be right up your alley, Leo. It forms a beneficial angle with your sun and bolsters all the qualities for which you're known and loved—warmth, compassion, flair for drama, ability to make friends with just about anyone.

This transit should bring about sudden, exciting change in your life. New opportunities for creative self-expression surface, and you find yourself feeling more free and buoyant than you have in years. You meet stimulating people, individuals who may be geniuses in their fields and who prove helpful to you in some way. There could be romance and love with this transit too, Leo. So many intriguing individuals are entering your life now that you'll have your pick!

You may travel abroad unexpectedly, for business, pleasure, or both. You might go to college, grad school, law school. You're looking for new knowledge and insights and could study astrology, the I Ching, tarot, or other divination systems. This is a great period to set up a regular exercise regimen if you don't have one already. You also should consider yoga.

Virgo ♍

Mutable earth sign

You're the perfectionist of the zodiac, detail oriented and precise in just about everything you do. These qualities prove helpful during the Uranus transit through Aries, which occurs in your solar eighth house. Let's take a closer, more detailed look.

Sudden, unexpected events and experiences may force you to break away from limitations and restrictions that make you feel trapped. These limitations and restrictions were either self-imposed or imposed on you by others. Whatever the source, you now make decisions to break free of these limitations. You feel as if the restrictions are eating away at your soul. If a job has made you feel this way, then you take definite steps to get out of the situation. If a relationship is the source of your feelings, then you end it. One way or another, restrictions become intolerable, and you bust free.

Since the eighth house represents joint resources, your partner's income may rise or fall suddenly, unexpectedly. You could inherit money. It's an excellent time to get out of debt. In fact, debt may be another limitation that you find intolerable.

Any new romance that comes your way could be highly sexual and have a deeply intuitive component to it.

Libra ♎

Cardinal air sign

One of your greatest strengths is your ability to interact with people. It's not just a social thing for you, either. You generally enjoy people and exploring what makes them tick. This ability will serve you well through the Uranus transit in Aries.

Uranus is now moving in opposition to your sun, through your solar seventh house, so your closest partnerships—romantic and business—are impacted. Sudden, unexpected events bring about the beginning and end of partnerships and force you to stand up for who you are and what you really believe. In doing so, you break free of restrictions that have become unbearable.

This transit may seem harsh at times. It appears that stuff is happening *to* you, that the universe is ganging up against you. But what's actually happening is that energies you have repressed over the years are now scrambling for release. Any relationship that ends under this transit—through death or otherwise—does so because it has served its purpose. Relationships that begin during this transit are apt to be exciting, different in some way, and stimulating mentally, emotionally, and spiritually.

To navigate this transit successfully, it's best not to resist events. Just go with the flow. Your creative self-expression during this period is important. Express what you feel when you feel it. If you hold your emotions inside, it could result in health problems or accidents. One way or another, the emotions find expression. Keep in mind that the whole purpose of this transit is to free you.

Scorpio ♏

Fixed water sign

Your greatest strengths are your uncanny intuition and ability to delve deeply for answers. During the Uranus transit through Aries, these qualities are heightened.

This transit is about freedom—from restrictions and limitations in any area of your life that prevent you from evolving creatively, spiritually, emotionally. As a fixed water sign, you probably don't like change any more than your fixed-sign brothers—Taurus, Leo, and Aquarius. But change you must. It's easier if you can learn to embrace change rather than resist it so that it isn't thrust on you.

Since this transit occurs in your solar sixth house, the

area most likely to be impacted is your daily work routine and health. The possible scenarios depend on how rigid, routine, or boring your daily work is; whether you stick to this work primarily because it's comfortable; and whether or not you enjoy what you're doing. The health aspect depends on how well you take care of yourself and your beliefs about health. In other words, if you believe that people get colds every winter, then you probably will get a cold every winter. So take inventory of your beliefs, Scorpio!

Sagittarius ♐
Mutable fire sign

The Uranus transit through fellow fire sign Aries is an adventure for you, exciting and stimulating, with the kind of surprises you enjoy. It occurs in your solar fifth house of love and romance, creativity, and children. It's likely that romantic relationships begin and end suddenly, that your creativity is taking you in new directions, and that everything you enjoy takes on a brighter patina.

With Uranus in Aries forming a beneficial angle to your sun, you're able to become who you really are. Your creative self-expression shines forth, and new venues for creativity open up. You may find yourself involved in projects that are totally different from anything you've done before that prompt you to stretch your creativity in new ways.

In romance and love relationships that no longer serve your best interests will end, and new relationships that are more in line with your needs and desires will begin. Your sexuality is heightened, and sex may be a large component of any relationship that begins during this seven-year transit.

If you're a Sadge who enjoys travel—and you probably are, many of your sign do—then you'll be doing more of it during this transit. You might move too, if you find a place that is more in line with the new you.

Capricorn ♑
Cardinal earth sign

You're known for your focus, clarity about your goals, and ability to plow through any obstacle you encounter. All of these traits will serve you well during the Uranus transit through Aries. However, since this transit forms a challenging angle to your sun sign, you may have to make some adjustments in your approach, Capricorn.

During this transit any limitations or restrictions that are self-imposed or imposed on you by others will become unbearable. Sudden, unexpected events will create situations that enable you to break free of these restrictions, but the events seem to come out of nowhere and may be upsetting. The transit occurs in your solar fourth house—your domestic environment—so let's take a look at some possible scenarios:

Your parents move in with you.

Your employer is relocating, and if you want to keep your job, you have to move too.

Your partner or spouse is laid off work, and you have to sell your home and move to a smaller place.

Your parents get divorced, and you have to relocate.

You get the idea here. The fourth house represents the foundation of your life, the most intimate and personal part of who you are. For most of us, changes in this area can be deeply unsettling. Any part of this area that has grown stale, rigid, or routine will be affected. But if your home life is vibrant and exciting, then it won't be impacted. Just try to be as flexible as you can; embrace the changes that come your way. This transit is intended to free you emotionally, creatively, and spiritually.

Aquarius ♒

Fixed air sign

The Uranus transit through Aries forms a beneficial angle to your sun, so you've got plenty to look forward to, Aquarius. This transit occurs in your solar third house, which represents communication, your conscious mind, neighborhood and neighbors, siblings, daily life, travel. This area is where you're apt to experience all the excitement of this transit. Let's take a closer look.

At this time your consciousness is expanding, leaping outward, seeking new ideas, exploring different belief systems and lifestyles. You may move quite suddenly and unexpectedly, but it turns out to be beneficial for you. You may undertake creative projects that are outside your usual talents and abilities and discover a new facet of your personality. This period is all about trying the new and unexplored, about adventures in consciousness and communication.

It's the ideal time to start a blog, build a Web site,

or write a novel or other book. Get involved in community activities. Get out and meet new people. Network. Enjoy yourself. Uranus, the planet that rules your sign, won't disappoint you during this transit. To enhance the effects of this transit, strive to be flexible, to go with the flow.

Pisces)(
Mutable water sign

Like your mutable siblings—Gemini, Virgo, and Sagittarius—you don't have any problem with change. But because this transit occurs in a fire sign, Aries, your solar second house of finances, it's a good idea to take an honest look at your finances.

How do you earn your living? Is it in line with your beliefs and ideals? Has it grown stale, are you just going through the motions? If so, then Uranus in Aries may shake up your financial picture to the point where you must take steps to rectify things. You may take a second job, for instance, thinking the additional income will help, but then that job turns into the job of your dreams. Or you could get laid off, and it turns out to be the best thing that ever happened to you, just the nudge you need to launch your own business.

Your imagination and intuition prove helpful during this transit. Be sure to listen to your intuition and allow your imagination to take you places you've never been before. Nothing is too wild to try, too *out there* to consider. However, here are some suggestions for making this transit a bit easier: pay cash for everything, get rid of your credit card debt, stick to a budget.

CHAPTER 2

Astro Basics

On the day you were born, what was the weather like? If you were born at night, had the moon already risen? Was it full or the shape of a Cheshire cat's grin? Was the delivery ward quiet or bustling with activity? Unless your mom or dad has a very good memory, you'll probably never know the full details. But there's one thing you can know for sure: on the day you were born the sun was located in a particular zone of the zodiac, an imaginary 360-degree belt that circles the Earth. The belt is divided into twelve 30-degree portions called signs.

If you were born between July 23 and August 22, then the sun was passing through the sign of Leo, so we say that your sun sign is Leo. Each of the twelve signs has distinct attributes and characteristics. Leos, for instance, love being the center of attention. They're warm, compassionate people with a flair for the dramatic. Virgos, born between August 23 and September 22, are perfectionists with discriminating intellects and a genius for details. Capricorns, born between December 22 and January 19, are the worker bees of the zodiac, serious minded, ambitious, industrious.

How Signs Are Classified

As you probably gathered from the first chapter, the twelve signs are categorized according to element and quality or modality. The first category, element, reads like a basic science lesson—fire, earth, air, and water— and describes the general physical characteristics of the signs.

Fire signs—Aries, Leo, Sagittarius—are warm, dynamic individuals who are always passionate about what they do.

Earth signs—Taurus, Virgo, Capricorn—are the builders of the zodiac, practical and efficient, grounded in everything they do.

Air signs—Gemini, Libra, Aquarius—are people who live mostly in the world of ideas. They are terrific communicators.

Water signs—Cancer, Scorpio, Pisces—live through their emotions, imaginations, and intuitions.

The second category describes how each sign operates in the physical world, how adaptable it is to circumstances.

Cardinal signs—Aries, Cancer, Libra, Capricorn—are initiators. These people are active, impatient, restless. They're great at starting things, but unless a project or relationship holds their attention, they lose interest and may not finish what they start.

Fixed signs—Taurus, Leo, Scorpio, Aquarius—are deliberate, controlled, resolute. These individuals tend to move more slowly than cardinal signs, are often stubborn, and resist change. They seek roots and stability and are always in the game for the long haul. They aren't quitters.

Mutable signs — Gemini, Virgo, Sagittarius, Pisces — are adaptable. These people are flexible, changeable, communicative. They don't get locked into rigid patterns or belief systems.

SUN SIGNS

Sign	Date	Element	Quality
Aries ♈	March 21–April 19	Fire	Cardinal
Taurus ♉	April 20–May 20	Earth	Fixed
Gemini ♊	May 21–June 21	Air	Mutable
Cancer ♋	June 22–July 22	Water	Cardinal
Leo ♌	July 23–August 22	Fire	Fixed
Virgo ♍	August 23–September 22	Earth	Mutable
Libra ♎	September 23–October 22	Air	Cardinal
Scorpio ♏	October 23–November 21	Water	Fixed
Sagittarius ♐	November 22–December 21	Fire	Mutable
Capricorn ♑	December 22–January 19	Earth	Cardinal
Aquarius ♒	January 20–February 18	Air	Fixed
Pisces ♓	February 19–March 20	Water	Mutable

The Planets

The planets in astrology are the players who make things happen. They're the characters in the story of your life. This story always begins with the sun, the giver of life.

Your sun sign describes your self-expression, your primal energy, the essence of who you are. It's the archetypal pattern of your Self. When you know another person's sun sign, you already have a great deal of information about that person. Let's say you're a Taurus who has just started dating a Gemini. How compatible are you?

On the surface, it wouldn't seem that you have much in common. Taurus is a fixed earth sign; Gemini is a mutable air sign. Taurus is persistent, stubborn, practical, a cultivator as opposed to an initiator. Gemini is a chameleon, a communicator, social, with a mind as quick as lightning. Taurus is ruled by Venus, which governs the arts, money, beauty, love, and romance. Gemini is ruled by Mercury, which governs communication and travel. There doesn't seem to be much common ground. But before we write off this combination, let's look a little deeper.

Suppose the Taurus has Mercury in Gemini, and the Gemini has Venus in Taurus? This would mean that the Taurus and Gemini each have their rulers in the other person's sign. They probably communicate well and enjoy travel and books (Mercury) and would see eye to eye on romance, art, and music (Venus). They might get along so well, in fact, that they collaborate on creative projects.

Each of us is also influenced by the other nine planets (the sun and moon are treated like planets in astrology) and the signs they were transiting when we were born. Suppose our Taurus and Gemini have the same moon sign? The moon rules our inner needs, emotions and intuition, and all that makes us feel secure within ourselves. Quite often compatible moon signs can overcome even the most glaring difference in sun signs because the two people share similar emotions.

In the section on predictions your sun sign always

takes center stage, and every prediction is based on the movement of the transiting planets in relation to your sun sign. Let's say you're a Sagittarius. Between October 7 and November 5 this year Venus will be transiting your sign. What does this mean for you? Well, since Venus rules—among other things—romance, you can expect your love life to pick up significantly during these weeks. Other people will find you attractive and be more open to your ideas, and you'll radiate a certain charisma. Your creative endeavors will move full steam ahead.

The planets table provides an overview of the planets and the signs that they rule. Keep in mind that the moon is the swiftest-moving planet, changing signs about every two and a half days, and that Pluto is the snail of the zodiac, taking as long as thirty years to transit a single sign. Although the faster-moving planets—the moon, Mercury, Venus, and Mars—have an impact on our lives, it's the slow pokes—Uranus, Neptune, and Pluto—that bring about the most profound influence and change. Jupiter and Saturn fall between the others in terms of speed. This year Jupiter spends the first six months in Gemini, then enters Cancer on June 25 and doesn't leave that sign until July 16, 2014.

In the section on predictions the most frequent references are to the transits of Mercury, Venus, and Mars and the movements of the transiting moon.

Now glance through the planets table. When a sign is in parentheses, it means the planet corules that sign. This assignation dates back to when we thought there were only seven planets in the solar system. But since there were still twelve signs, some of the planets had to do double duty!

THE PLANETS

Planet	Rules	Attributes of Planet
Sun ☉	Leo	self-expression, primal energy, creative ability, ego, individuality
Moon ☽	Cancer	emotions, intuition, mother or wife, security
Mercury ☿	Gemini, Virgo	intellect, mental acuity, communication, logic, reasoning, travel, contracts
Venus ♀	Taurus, Libra	love, romance, beauty, artistic instincts, the arts, music, material and financial resources
Mars ♂	Aries (Scorpio)	physical and sexual energy, aggression, drive
Jupiter ♃	Sagittarius (Pisces)	luck, expansion, success, prosperity, growth, creativity, spiritual interests, higher education, law
Saturn ♄	Capricorn (Aquarius)	laws of physical universe, discipline, responsibility, structure, karma, authority
Uranus ♅	Aquarius	individuality, genius, eccentricity, originality, science, revolution
Neptune ♆	Pisces	visionary self, illusions, what's hidden, psychic ability, dissolution of ego boundaries, spiritual insights, dreams

Planet	Rules	Attributes of Planet
Pluto ♀ ♇	Scorpio	the darker side, death, sex, regeneration, rebirth, profound and permanent change, transformation

Houses and Rising Signs

In the instant you drew your first breath, one of the signs of the zodiac was just passing over the eastern horizon. Astrologers refer to this as the rising sign or ascendant. It's what makes your horoscope unique. Think of your ascendant as the front door of your horoscope, the place where you enter into this life and begin your journey.

Your ascendant is based on the exact moment of your birth, and the other signs follow counterclockwise. If you have Taurus rising, for example, that is the cusp of your first house. The cusp of the second would be Gemini, of the third Cancer, and so on around the horoscope circle in a counterclockwise direction. Each house governs a particular area of life, which is outlined below.

The best way to find out your rising sign is to have your horoscope drawn up by an astrologer. For those of you with access to the Internet, though, there are several sites that provide free birth horoscopes: www.astro.com and www.cafeastrology.com are two good ones.

In a horoscope the ascendant (cusp of the first house), IC (cusp of the fourth house), descendant (cusp of the seventh house), and MC (cusp of the tenth house) are considered to be the most critical angles. Any planets that fall close to these angles are extremely important in the overall astrological picture of who you are. By the same token, planets that fall in the first, fourth, seventh, and tenth houses are also considered to be important.

Now here's a rundown on what the houses mean.

Ascendant or Rising: The First of Four Important Critical Angles in a Horoscope

- How other people see you
- How you present yourself to the world
- Your physical appearance

First House, Personality

- Early childhood
- Your ego
- Your body type and how you feel about your body
- General physical health
- Defense mechanisms
- Your creative thrust

Second House, Personal Values

- How you earn and spend your money
- Your personal values
- Your material resources and assets
- Your attitudes and beliefs toward money
- Your possessions and your attitude toward those possessions
- Your self-worth
- Your attitudes about creativity

Third House, Communication and Learning

- Personal expression
- Intellect and mental attitudes and perceptions
- Siblings, neighbors, and relatives
- How you learn
- School until college
- Reading, writing, teaching
- Short trips (the grocery store versus Europe in seven days)
- Earth-bound transportation
- Creativity as a communication device

IC or Fourth House Cusp: The Second Critical Angle in a Horoscope

- Sign on IC describes the qualities and traits of your home during early childhood
- Describes roots of your creative abilities and talents

Fourth House, Your Roots

- Personal/domestic environment
- Your home
- Your attitudes toward family
- Early childhood conditioning
- Real estate
- Your nurturing parent

Some astrologers say this house belongs to Mom or her equivalent in your life, others say it belongs to

Dad or his equivalent. It makes sense to us that it's Mom because the fourth house is ruled by the moon, which rules mothers. But in this day and age, when parental roles are in flux, the only hard and fast rule is that the fourth belongs to the parent who nurtures you most of the time.

- The conditions at the end of your life
- Early childhood support of your creativity and interests

Fifth House, Children and Creativity

- Kids, your first-born in particular
- Love affairs, romance
- What you enjoy
- Creative ability
- Gambling and speculation
- Pets

Traditionally, pets belong in the sixth house. But that definition stems from the days when "pets" were chattel. These days we don't even refer to them as pets. They are animal companions who bring us pleasure.

Sixth House, Work and Responsibility

- Day-to-day working conditions and environment
- Competence and skills
- Your experience of employees and employers
- Duty to work, to employees
- Health and the daily maintenance of your health

Descendant/Seventh House Cusp: The Third Critical Angle in a Horoscope

- The sign on the house cusp describes the qualities sought in intimate or business relationships
- Describes qualities of creative partnerships

Seventh House, Partnerships and Marriage

- Marriage
- Marriage partner
- Significant others
- Business partnerships
- Close friends
- Open enemies
- Contracts

Eighth House: Transformation

- Sexuality as transformation
- Secrets
- Death, taxes, inheritances, insurance, mortgages, and loans
- Resources shared with others
- Your partner's finances
- The occult (read: astrology, reincarnation, UFOs, everything weird and strange)
- Your hidden talents
- Psychology
- Life-threatening illnesses
- Your creative depths

Ninth House, Worldview

- Philosophy and religion
- The law, courts, judicial system
- Publishing
- Foreign travels and cultures
- College, graduate school
- Spiritual beliefs
- Travel abroad

MC or Cusp of Tenth House: The Fourth Critical Angle in a Horoscope

- Sign on cusp of MC describes qualities you seek in a profession
- Your public image
- Your creative and professional achievements

Tenth House, Profession and Career

- Public image as opposed to a job that merely pays the bills (sixth house)
- Your status and position in the world
- The authoritarian parent and authority in general
- People who hold power over you
- Your public life
- Your career/profession

Eleventh House, Ideals and Dreams

- Peer groups
- Social circles (your writers' group, your mother's bridge club)

- Your dreams and aspirations
- How you can realize your dreams

Twelfth House, Personal Unconscious

- Power you have disowned that must be claimed again
- Institutions—hospitals, prisons, nursing homes—and what is hidden
- What you must confront this time around, your karma, issues brought in from other lives
- Psychic gifts and abilities
- Healing talents
- What you give unconditionally

In the section on predictions you'll find references to transiting planets moving into certain houses. These houses are actually solar houses that are created by putting your sun sign on the ascendant. This technique is how most predictions are made for the general public rather than for specific individuals.

Lunations

Every year there are twelve new moons and twelve full moons, with some years having thirteen full moons. The extra full moon is called the Blue Moon. New moons are typically when we should begin new projects, set new goals, seek new opportunities. They're times for beginnings. They usher in new opportunities according to house and sign.

Two weeks after each new moon, there's a full moon.

This is the time of harvest, fruition, when we reap what we've sown.

Whenever a new moon falls in your sign, take time to brainstorm what you would like to achieve during weeks and months until the full moon falls in your sign. These goals can be in any area of your life. Or you can simply take the time on each new moon to set up goals and strategies for what you would like to achieve or manifest during the next two weeks—until the full moon—or until the next new moon.

Here's a list of all the new moons and full moons during 2013. The asterisk beside any new-moon entry indicates a solar eclipse; the asterisk next to a full-moon entry indicates a lunar eclipse.

LUNATIONS OF 2013

New Moons

January 11—Capricorn
February 10—Aquarius
March 11—Pisces
April 10—Aries
*May 9—Taurus
June 8—Gemini
July 8—Cancer
August 6—Leo
September 5—Virgo
October 4—Libra
*November 3—Scorpio
December 2—Sagittarius

Full Moons

January 26—Leo
February 25—Virgo
March 27—Libra
*April 25—Scorpio
*May 25—Sagittarius
June 23—Capricorn
July 22—Aquarius
August 20—Aquarius
September 19—Pisces
*October 18—Aries
November 17—Taurus
December 17—Gemini

Every year there are two lunar and two solar eclipses, separated from each other by about two weeks. Lunar eclipses tend to deal with emotional issues and our internal world and often bring an emotional issue to the surface related to the sign and house in which the eclipse falls. They can also result in news. Solar eclipses deal with events and often enable us to see something that has eluded us. They also symbolize beginnings and endings.

Read more about eclipses in the Big Picture for your sign for 2013. I also recommend Celeste Teal's excellent book, *Eclipses*.

Mercury Retrograde

Every year Mercury—the planet that symbolizes communication and travel—turns retrograde three times. During these periods our travel plans often go awry, communication breaks down, computers go berserk, cars or appliances develop problems. You get the idea. Things in our daily lives don't work as smoothly as we would like.

Here are some guidelines to follow for Mercury retrogrades:

Try not to travel. But if you have to, be flexible and think of it as an adventure. If you're stuck overnight in an airport in Houston or Atlanta, though, the adventure part of this could be a stretch.

Don't sign contracts—unless you don't mind revisiting them when Mercury is direct again.

Communicate as succinctly and clearly as possible.

Back up all computer files. Use an external hard drive and/or a flash drive. If you've had a computer crash, you already know how frustrating it can be to reconstruct your files.

Don't buy expensive electronics. Expensive anything.

Don't submit manuscripts, screenplays, pitch ideas, or launch new projects.

Revise, rewrite, rethink, review.

In the overview for each sign, check out the dates for this year's Mercury retrogrades and how these retrogrades are likely to impact you. Do the same for eclipses.

Other Retrogrades

Every planet except the sun and moon turns retrograde. So let's look at the retrogrades that will occur in 2013.

Venus: December 21, 2013, to January 31, 2014. When Venus is retrograde, your personal relationships often suffer from miscommunication, your love life is bumpy, romance can be withheld or minimized.

Mars: No retrogrades this year for Mars!

Jupiter: January 30 to November 7. Ouch. It's troublesome to have the planet of luck and expansion retrograde for so long. During this period your finances may be depressed, your luck factor isn't operating at full potential, and there could be setbacks or delays with publishing and educational ventures.

Saturn: February 18 to July 7. During this retrograde you discover which structures in your life need bolstering. Profits may be depressed.

Uranus: July 17 to December 17. Upheavals and changes occur within your inner life. You may not be quite as sharp and on top of things.

Neptune: June 6 to November 13. Your creativity and your ability to envision what you desire are limited in some way.

Pluto: April 12 to September 20. You may feel powerless or unmotivated in some area of your life.

CHAPTER 3

Romance, Love, and Creativity in 2013

Even during a year of transformation we still fall in love and get married, our creative muses are still whispering in our ears, our lives march on. For some of us our greatest transformation this year will unfold through romance, love, and creative ventures. So let's take a closer look at how each sun sign approaches love and romance and what types of creative activities they might be able to turn into gold.

Aries

Your passions are legendary. You're impulsive when it comes to matters of the heart and tend to leap in with both feet and ask questions later. Once you're involved you're involved completely and totally and want your partner to declare his or her undying love for you. The problem with this approach occurs when your partner doesn't feel the same way you do. Then jealousy and possessiveness creep in, Aries, and things can get muddled quickly.

Your freedom and independence are paramount to

your happiness, so you need a partner who understands and respects your space. But because you're a stranger to compromise, a vital part of any relationship, you may find intimate relationships challenging. Once you're involved, your passions are fierce and can easily topple into the dark extremes of jealousy, possessiveness, suspicion.

Your entrepreneurial and fearless spirit enjoys a partner who can compete with you on any level—on those long hikes into the wilderness, in the boardroom, in the classroom, in the garage out back where you're building your newest invention. You get the idea here, right, Aries? Boredom is your nemesis. So which signs are good matches for you? Let's take a closer look at some of the possibilities.

Sagittarius. This fellow fire sign will give you all the freedom you crave—and then some. She'll match you joke for joke, drink for drink. If she's the physical type, and many of them are, she'll match you on those hikes. But for a Sadge those hikes may be in some far-flung spot like Tibet. Like you, Sadge pushes herself, but she's more adaptable than you are. Sometimes she may come off like a know-it-all. But overall this combination holds great promise.

Gemini. This air sign's wit, versatility, and ability to talk about virtually anything appeal to you. He's generally not possessive, either, a major plus when you're in one of your darker moods. His mind is sharp and lightning quick, and he probably has a vast, complicated network of friends and acquaintances. Also appealing. So what're the negatives? Gemini generally isn't as independent as you are and may spend more time with his friends than he does with you. But overall this combination is lively, fun, and never boring.

Leo. Another fire sign. On the surface it looks like a good match. Leo possesses an infinite capacity for enjoyment, which appeals to you. But she also loves having center stage—not just sometimes, but most of the time—and that can be a major turnoff for you.

Libra, Aquarius. Libra is your opposite sign. The match could be fantastic because you balance each other. Where you're the loner, she's the social butterfly. You're independent, she's a networker with more friends than a hive has bees. Whether this works or not depends on the signs of your natal moons, ascendants, and Venus. You and Aquarius could be a winning combination. His independence matches yours, he's as sharp as the proverbial tack, and he pulls no punches in expressing what he wants, when he wants it. Downside? He may not be as physical or competitive and lives much of his life in his head.

What about another *Aries*? Depends on the signs of your moons. Strictly on the basis of sun signs, you're both so independent the relationship may never get off the ground!

Creatively, your interests span the spectrum of possibilities. So take your greatest passion and then study the market to find out how you might fill any gap that you identify. You excel at going where no one else dares to venture, Aries.

Taurus

As a sensual earth sign you love beautiful surroundings, good food, art, music, books. You tend to keep things to yourself, so a lot goes on beneath the surface that others don't see. You usually don't leap into a relationship, like Aries, but test the waters, discovering the other person's interests, passions, seeking commonalities in worldviews. Once you do get involved you're a considerate, loving, and sensual partner who expects the same level of commitment in return.

You're a stable individual, grounded and practical, but many of you have a deeper interest in the unknown, the unseen, the mysterious. If you find a partner who shares that interest in esoteric ideas, then you can overlook things in the relationship that may not work exactly as you would like. Communication, Taurus, is key for you.

You aren't into drama, artifice, flamboyance—not for yourself and not in a partner either. But you enjoy a partner who is physically attractive or who has a particular artistic gift that you appreciate—music, art, a way with words, anything that appeals to your senses.

If you're a Taurus who is into sports and health, and many of them are, then a health-conscious partner is a major plus. But there's another side to you too, an inner mystic, a quiet, observant Buddha who remains calm and centered, in tune with unseen forces. You would do well with a partner who possesses those qualities as well.

Leo, Sagittarius, Aries. Unless you have a moon, rising, or Venus in one of those signs, the fire signs probably won't work for you. Too much drama, boisterous behavior, and anger to suit your tastes.

Virgo, Capricorn. Fellow earth signs. Virgo could be the ticket. She's as practical as you are and, in many instances, just as mystical. Capricorn is focused and as physical as you are, but may not be as mystically in-clined.

Scorpio. Your opposite sign, so there may be a good balance. She's secretive and can be vengeful, but she's just as mystical as you are.

On the creative front you're in for the long haul. You aren't a quitter. Once you uncover your passion, you go for it big time and never give up.

Gemini

For you seduction begins with the mind, with ideas. Any prospective partner that fails to interest you in-tellectually doesn't remain long on your radar. You're the consummate communicator of the zodiac, the net-worker, so any relationship in which you're involved must have that communication component. Other-wise it probably won't last.

You're up front about what you feel, but those feel-ings could change at a moment's notice, a dichotomy that can be confusing to a partner. And to everyone else around you, for that matter. No wonder your sign is represented by the twins.

For you everything starts with a single burning question: *why?* You then set about finding out why and in the course of your journey may be distracted by a million other pieces of information that are even-tually integrated into your quest. This means, of course, that your journey toward the why of the origi-nal question may not end in *this* lifetime! So you need a partner whose curiosity matches your own.

Sagittarius, Aries. Sadge is your opposite sign. He matches you in curiosity, but may not be up to snuff in other areas. With Aries there's never a dull moment. She's a match for your quickness and wit, but may not have the curiosity you do about other people.

Libra and Aquarius. Usually compatible in that both signs value information and communication.

Water signs. Oddly, Pisces might be a good match because it's the only other sign represented by two of something. And his imagination will appeal to you.

Creatively, you excel at anything that involves communication. Better dust off that novel, Gemini, and start rewriting!

Cancer

In romance it's always about feelings first—not the mind, not even the body, but *emotions*. Your partner has to be as dedicated to her inner world as you are to yours, so that your inner worlds can, well, *merge*. That's the ideal. Yet because you're a cardinal sign, like Aries, Libra, and Capricorn, there's a certain independence in you that demands emotional space. Contradictory, but not to you.

Despite your emotional depth, you tend to avoid confrontations. Like the crab that symbolizes your sign you retreat into your shell at the first sign of trouble. Yet how can you smooth out anything in a relationship if you can't discuss disagreements? It's as if you expect disagreements to be ironed out telepathically. If that's true, then your best matches romantically are probably other water signs. Let's take a deeper look.

Pisces, Scorpio. Both signs are as psychic as you are but in different ways. Pisces is the softer of the two signs, dreamier. Scorpio might overwhelm you but gives you the emotional space you need.

Taurus. A good match. This earth sign helps you to ground yourself in the real world and gives you emotional space—maybe more than you need!

Capricorn, Virgo. Cappy is your opposite sign, so the possibility of balance is there. Virgo might be too picky for your tastes but shows you how to communicate verbally.

Air signs? Fire signs? Not so good, unless you have a moon, ascendant, Venus, or Mars in one of those signs.

Creatively, you excel at anything in which you can use your intuition and emotional power.

Leo

You've got enough passion for all the other signs in the zodiac—and then some. That passion is often linked to the attention of others, which probably explains why so many actors and actresses have a Leo sun, moon, or ascendant. Your life is about drama, and the higher the drama the deeper your passion. It's that passion that busts through obstacles, that burns a path toward where you want to go in both life and love.

Your compassion extends to anyone in a tough situation—or to any creature that needs love and reassurance that we humans aren't heartless. So let's be real here. Your partner, whoever he or she is, probably has to love animals the way you do. Even if there are twenty strays in your backyard, your partner must be amenable to the idea that you feed the multitudes. Not an easy request, says the universe. But there are some strong possibilities.

Sagittarius, Aries. Fellow fire signs. Sadge, symbolized by a creature that is half human and half horse, usually has animal companions—not pets, but *companions.* There's a big difference. She's your match in the compassion area. She understands your need to connect to an audience, but she may not stick around to be a part of that audience. The energy match with Aries is great. But unless you've got a moon, ascendant, or Venus in Aries, she may not shower you—or your animal companions—with enough attention.

Gemini, Libra. These two air signs could be excellent matches for you, Leo. You'll enjoy Gemini's lively intellect and Libra's artistic sensibilities.

Creatively, you excel at anything connected to drama, fashion, politics.

Virgo

You're the absolute master of details. You collect massive amounts of information, sift through it all with an eye for what works and what doesn't, and toss out everything that is extraneous. Your quest for perfection is never compromised. It's evident in the inner work you do, honing your own psyche, and in everything you take on in the external world. These qualities can make a romantic partnership somewhat challenging because your partner goes under the same microscope that everything else does.

You're a layered individual and benefit from a partner who understands that and knows how to peel away those layers without making you feel vulnerable or exposed. A partner who enjoys every single one of those layers. So who's your best match?

Taurus and Capricorn. Fellow earth signs. Taurus takes all the time the relationship needs to peel away the layers of your personality so she could find the gold at your core. She's patient, resolute, determined. Capricorn might consider the relationship as just one more challenge to be conquered but could provide a nice balance to your penchant for details.

Cancer, Scorpio. These two water signs complement you. Cancer grasps who you are emotionally but may not be as willing as you are to discuss elements of the relationship. Since your sign is ruled by Mercury, the planet of communication, that could be a drawback. Scorpio's emotional intensity could be overwhelming but he'll be delighted to peel away the layers of your personality!

Gemini. Even though air and earth aren't usually compatible, Gemini and Virgo share Mercury as a ruler. Communication in this combination is likely to be strong and fluid, with a constant exchange of ideas.

On the creative front, your specialty is details: editor, writer, mystic, researcher, anything involving health and medicine.

Libra

There's a certain duality in your psychological makeup that isn't mentioned very often. It's not due to a penchant for secrecy or deviousness but to a reluctance to hurt anyone's feelings. As a result you often find yourself paralyzed by indecision. *Who do I really love? A or B?* Since you don't want to hurt either person, you maintain both relationships and make yourself and everyone around you absolutely nuts.

You have a need for harmony and balance in relationships. You dislike confrontation and dissension, so all too often you surrender to your partner's wants at your own expense. So which signs are good matches for you?

Gemini, Aquarius. Fellow air signs understand your psychological makeup. Gemini experiences some of the same duality that you do but for different reasons. He isn't bothered by dichotomies, since his own life is predicated on them. He appeals to that part of you that needs to communicate honestly. Aquarius may be a bit too rigid for you, insisting that you bend to his desires, but the depth and breadth of his vision attract you at a visceral level.

Sagittarius, Leo, Aries. Any of the fire signs could be an excellent match. Sagittarius never bores you and enjoys you for *who you are*. Leo may want more attention than you're willing to give, but her warmth and compassion will delight you. You and Aries, your opposite sign, balance each other.

Taurus, Virgo, Capricorn. Of the three earth signs, Taurus is probably the best match because you share Venus as a ruler. That means you have similar tastes in music and art and probably share some of the same attitudes and beliefs about money.

Creatively, Libras do well at music, art, writing— anything in the arts—but also excel with people.

Scorpio

As the most emotionally intense sign of the zodiac and one of the most psychic, your powerful and magnetic personality can intimidate even heads of state.

Your life patterns are about breaking taboos, digging deeper, looking for the absolute bottom line in whatever you do, in any relationship in which you become involved. You feel and intuit your way through life, and your partner must understand that.

All of this brooding and mulling takes place in the privacy of your own head. The side you show others is lighter, funny, with a dry wit that can charm, seduce, or spar with the best of them. Yet inside you're always asking, *What motivates him? What secrets does he have?* Given the complexities of your personality, which signs are most compatible with yours?

Pisces, Cancer. Of these two water signs, Pisces matches you in raw intuitive ability but may be too indecisive to suit you long term. Cancer can be just as secretive as you, but unless you've got a moon or rising in Cancer, this sign could be too clingy.

Taurus, Virgo, Capricorn. The earth signs are compatible matches. Taurus, your opposite sign, brings sensuality to your sexuality and helps to dispel your suspicions about other people's motives. Her earthiness grounds your psychic ability. Virgo's discerning and gentle nature mitigates your emotional intensity. Capricorn's determination appeals to that same quality in you.

Fire signs? *Leos* and Scorpios are both fixed signs, and there seems to be something between them that is powerful. Look at Leo Bill Clinton and Scorpio Hillary.

On the creative front, you're good at anything that enables you to use your intuition and your investigative skills.

Sagittarius

You're so multifaceted, with so many different talents, that a relationship presents certain dilemmas, e.g., commitment to another person. It's so much easier to commit to, well, your own interests! Also there's that little ole thing called personal freedom, which you value every bit as much as Aries.

Like Libra, there's a curious duality in your makeup, best explained perhaps by the symbol for your sign—the mythological centaur. Half horse, half human, this figure might be defined as the wild woman (or man) versus the conformist. A part of you operates from gut instinct and the other part of you is acculturated. Which signs are your best matches?

Aries, Leo, Sagittarius. As remarked under the Aries section, a relationship with this sign may not go anywhere because you're both so independent. Aries might want to be in charge all the time, and you get fed up and hit the open road. Leo could be a terrific choice, particularly if one of you has a moon in the other's sun sign. Another Sadge would be intriguing.

Taurus, Virgo, Capricorn. Of these three earth signs, Capricorn is the best match. Even if she lacks your intuitive gifts, her focus, direction, and resolute determination equal yours. Taurus, your opposite sign, could also be a good match. You share a fascination with the paranormal, and your energies would balance each other.

Air signs? Water signs? Probably not, unless you have a moon, rising, or some other prominent planet in those signs.

You would excel at anything creative that is related to travel, publishing, and higher education.

Capricorn

You build relationships in the same careful way that you build everything else in your life—a brick at a time. A conversation here, a dinner there, a movie, a moonlit walk, an exchange of beliefs: you're methodical, consistent, disciplined. Pretty soon the foundation is solid, the chemistry is exactly right, and you know exactly what you want.

A relationship, of course, involves the human heart—not mortar and bricks—and that's where it may get tricky. You could discover that your methodical approach doesn't work as well in a relationship as it does with your career. Your success will depend to a certain extent on your compatibility with your partner.

Taurus, Virgo, Capricorn. Taurus' solidity and dependability appeal to you, and he's as private as you are. But his still waters run deep, and he may not express his emotions as readily as you would like. Yet the match would be a good one. Virgo understands what drives you. Another Capricorn—i.e., type A personality—would wear you out!

Scorpio, Pisces. While either of these water signs is compatible with your earth-sign sun, Pisces may too ambivalent for you, too indecisive. Scorpio, though, is a strong match. All that intensity appeals to you at a visceral level, your sex life would be fantastic, and you share a similar determination. *Cancer*, your opposite sign, might work if the Cancer has a moon or rising in your sign.

Fire signs? Air signs? Again, it depends on the distribution of fire- and air-sign planets in your natal chart.

Your creative interests are varied, and you approach them with the same methodical, relentless energy that you bring to other facets of your life. You build worlds, Capricorn—in software, writing, photography, dance, art.

Aquarius

In love and romance, as in life, your mind is your haven, your sanctuary, your sacred place. It's where everything begins for you. From your visionary, cutting edge ideas to your humanitarian causes and interests in the esoteric, you're a wild card, not easily pigeonholed. It doesn't make any difference to you whether your partner shares these interests, as long as he or she recognizes your right to pursue them.

There's a rebel in you that pushes against the status quo, and that's something your partner has to understand too. Your connections to people and to the world aren't easily grasped by others. Too weird, they think. Too out there. But that's fine. You understand who and what you are, and in the end that's all you need. So which signs are your best matches?

Gemini, Libra. Your air-sign *compadres* are excellent matches. Gemini suits your prodigious intellect, causes, and ideas. Good communication usually is a hallmark of this relationship, and Gemini is supportive of your causes. With Libra the focus is on relationships—yours and Libra's connection to five million others. But the right mix exists for a strong partnership. A relationship with another *Aquarius* could be challenging since you'll both insist you're right. But if you can move past that, you'll do fine. Another Aquarius may be like looking in the mirror 24/7. Not for the faint hearted.

Aries, Leo, Sagittarius. With these fire signs you enjoy the freedom to be your own person. Life with Aries is never boring, the conversation and adventures are stimulating, but he may not share your humanitarian and esoteric interests. Sagittarius loves your mind and insights, your idealism and rebellion against the establishment. Great compatibility overall. Leo is your opposite sign, suggesting a good balance between your head and his heart.

Earth or water signs? Only if you have prominent planets in either of those elements.

Your creative talents don't fit under any tidy category. They are as varied and different as your lifestyle and worldview. If you focus on just one of these talents, you can mine it for gold!

Pisces

It's true that your inner world is often more real and genuine to you than anything in the external world. The richness of your imagination, the breadth of your intuition — these qualities create a kind of seductive atmosphere that's tough to move beyond. But because you're a physical being in a physical world, who has to eat and sleep, work and function, who loves and triumphs and yearns, you have to move beyond it. So you do.

But always there's an inner tension, a kind of bewilderment, a constant questioning. *Where am I going? What am I doing? Do I really want to do this or that?* Your head and your heart are forever at odds, so no wonder your sign is symbolized by two fish moving in opposite directions. In romance and love this indecisiveness can be problematic. So which signs are most compatible for you?

Scorpio, Cancer. Scorpio's emotional intensity could overwhelm you, but he balances your indecisiveness with his unwavering commitment to a particular path. Intuitively, you're on the same page, a major plus. Cancer's innate gentleness appeals to you, and she appreciates you exactly as you are.

Taurus, Capricorn. These two earth signs appeal to you at a visceral level. Taurus' solid, grounded personality comforts that part of you that is so often torn between one direction and another. Her sensuality is also a major plus. Capricorn's singular vision and direction are mysteries to you, but there's much to learn from her. *Virgo*, your opposite sign, can bring balance.

Fire signs probably won't work for you unless you have a moon or rising in a fire sign. Of the air signs, *Gemini* is probably the most compatible for you. Since you're both symbolized by two of something — two fish, the twins — he understands your dichotomies.

With your imagination and psychic ability, the world really lies at your feet in a creative sense. All you have to do is decide which talent to nurture and then plug yourself into it and let your muse do the rest.

CHAPTER 4

Health and Fitness in 2013

Taking Responsibility for Your Own Health

In the U.S. more money per person is spent on health care than in any other country in the world. Yet life expectancy in this country ranks fiftieth, and the U.S. lags behind other wealthy nations in infant mortality. According to the Institute of Medicine, the United States is the only country in the world that doesn't ensure that all its citizens have coverage.

In the U.S. health insurance is controlled by private corporations whose bottom line is profit, not health. The only exceptions are government-run programs like Medicare, Medicaid, the Veterans' Administration, and some programs for children. If you followed the contentious health-care debate, you undoubtedly heard about death panels, government takeover of the health-care system, and other nonsense. One clip we remember was amusing: an older woman standing up at a Tea Party meeting, waving her sign—*No to Obama Care*—while she shouted, "Keep your hands off my Medicare!"

In the end, when the final bill went through Congress, there were some significant changes: mandated health insurance that begins in 2014, insurance companies can no longer deny coverage for preexisting conditions, and children can remain on their parents' health insurance until the age of twenty-six. But the bill didn't go far enough. Medicare for all would be the ideal.

Until insurance companies are removed from health care, the health care in this country will continue to be a discriminatory system. The real death panels will continue to be insurance companies who deny care for profit.

If nothing else, that debate and the reality of health care in this country should encourage you to take charge of your own health. Here are some simple suggestions:

1) *If you don't have a regular exercise routine yet, start one.* Pick something that you know you can do daily.

2) *Watch what you eat. Read the labels on the food you buy.* How much sodium is there in your favorite foods? How much cholesterol? Fats? Even organic foods have a high sodium content. The other day at Whole Foods we picked up some soy bacon and then turned the box over to look at the contents. For a single slice of soy bacon, the nutritional facts state:

Total fat—1 gram
No saturated or trans fat, no polyunsaturated or monounsaturated fats
Cholesterol—0 mg
Sodium—140 mg
Potassium—40 mg
No carbs, no sugar
Protein—2 g

That's a lot of sodium for a single skinny slice of soy bacon! Compare this to our favorite organic chicken sausage, however, which has 460 mg of sodium for a single link, and the soy bacon looks good. Once you get into the habit of reading the labels, you will be more careful in your selection of foods.

3) *Meditation and yoga are two healthy practices you might consider.* Meditation has been shown to: lower blood pressure and oxygen consumption, decrease respiratory rate, slow heart rate, reduce anxiety and stress, enhance the immune system. Yoga increases your physical flexibility—and eventually your emotional and mental flexibility as well. It helps to strengthen your body, improves muscle tone, improves posture, improves lung capacity because of the deep breathing involved, and reduces stress.

4) *Try various nutritional and vitamin programs.* Educate yourself. The Internet is filled with health and fitness Web sites.

5) *Try a homeopathic practitioner or acupuncturist before you run to your doctor for a prescription.*

If you were an alien watching the evening news and the drug commercials that sponsor it, you might get the impression that Americans are a sickly lot in search of the quickest fix. While drugs certainly have their place, more and more Americans are seeking alternative treatments for whatever ails them. From acupuncture to yoga and homeopathy, from vitamin regimens to nutritional programs, more and more of us are taking control over our own health and bodies.

6) *Take inventory of your beliefs.* If medical intuitives like Louise Hay and Carolyn Myss are correct, then our health is about more than just eating right

and getting sufficient exercise. It's also about our emotions, our inner worlds, our belief systems. How happy are you in your job? Your closest partnerships? Your friendships? Are you generally happy with the money you earn? What would you change about your life? Do you believe you have free will or that everything is destined? Is your mood generally upbeat? Do you feel you have choices? Do you feel empowered? By asking yourself these kinds of questions, you can glean a sense of your emotional state at any given time. And the state of your emotions may tell you a great deal about the state of your health.

Louise Hay, author of *You Can Heal Your Life* and founder of Hay House publishing, is a living testament to the impact of emotions on health. As a young woman she was diagnosed with vaginal cancer. The doctors wanted to operate, but Hay bought herself time—three months—by telling them she didn't have the money. She then took control of her treatment.

As a child who had been sexually abused at the age of five, it wasn't surprising to her that the cancer had shown up where it had. She knew that cancer was "a dis-ease of deep resentment that has been held for a long period of time until it literally eats away at the body." She felt that if she could change the mental pattern that had created the cancer, if she could release the patterns of resentment, then she could cure herself.

She set out a program for her treatment, and forgiveness was the top of her list. She also knew she had to "love and approve" of herself more. In addition she found a good therapist, nutritionist, and foot reflexologist, had colonics three times a week, and exercised. Her treatment is spelled out in her book. The end result? Within six months the doctors pronounced her free of cancer.

In her book there's an invaluable list: next to every ailment and disease is the probable emotional cause and the new thought pattern that will lead to healing. Her techniques may not be for everyone, but when dealing with health and fitness issues remember that medical science doesn't have all the answers, and you, in fact, may be your own best healer.

7) *Practice the art of appreciation. Expect the best from others.* If you can get into the habit of doing these two things, you're well ahead of the game in maintaining your health.

The Physical You

These descriptions fit both sun and rising signs. For a more complete look at the physical you, of course, your entire natal chart should be taken into account, with a particularly close look at the sign of your moon—the root of your emotions, the cradle of your inner world.

Aries

Rules: head and face

2013 Tip:

In this year of transformation transform yourself from the inside out, Aries. Start with your thoughts. Notice what you think throughout a given day. If you notice that a lot of negative thoughts surface, nudge them on their way by reaching for more positive ones.

Health and Fitness

Aries rules the head and face, so these areas are often the most vulnerable physically. Headaches, dizziness, and skin eruptions can be common. If you're an athletic Aries, then do more of whatever it is that you enjoy. Competitive sports? Great, go for it. Long-distance runner? Run farther. Gym? Double your time and your workout. Yoga once a week? Do it three times a week. One way or another you need to burn off your excessive energy, so that it doesn't turn inward and short-circuit your body!

As a cardinal fire sign you're an active person who gravitates toward daring, risky sports—mountain climbing, rappelling, bungee jumping, trekking through high mountainous regions, leaping out of airplanes. It's probably a great idea to have good health insurance or a Louise Hay attitude toward your health—*I'm attracting only magnificent experiences into my life.*

For maximum benefit you probably should try to eliminate red meat from your diet. Chicken and fish are fine, but a vegan diet would be best. Herbs like mustard, eye-bright, and bay are beneficial for you. Any antioxidant is helpful—particularly vitamins C, E, A or Lutein for your eyes, zinc, Co-Q10, Black Cohosh if you're a female in menopause, or Saw Palmetto if you're a man older than fifty. If you pull a muscle or throw your back out of whack, look for a good acupuncturist and avoid painkillers.

Taurus

Rules: neck, throat, cervical vertebrae

2013 Tip:

Since this is a year of transformation, start by communicating what you feel to someone you love. Don't take it for granted that the person knows how you feel.

Health and Fitness

Thanks to the sensuality of your sign, you may be a gourmet cook and enjoy rich foods. But because your metabolism may be somewhat slow, you benefit from daily exercise and moderation in your diet. In fact, moderation in all things is probably a good rule to follow.

As a fixed earth sign you benefit from any outdoor activity, and the more physical it is, the better it is for you. Hiking, skiing, windsurfing, biking are all excellent pursuits. You also benefit from any mind/body discipline like tai chi or yoga. The latter is especially good since it keeps you flexible, and that flexibility spills over into your attitudes and beliefs and the way you deal with situations and people. You probably enjoy puttering in a garden, but because you have such an artistic side, you don't just putter. You remake the garden into a work of art—fountains, bold colors, mysterious paths that twist through greenery and flowers. Once you include wind chimes and bird feeders, nature's music adds the finishing touches.

If your job entails long hours of sitting in front of a computer, your neck and shoulders may be more tense than usual. You would benefit through regular massage and hot tub soaks.

If you're the silent type of Taurus, then chances are you don't discuss your emotions. This tendency can cause health challenges if you keep anger or resentment bottled up inside you. Best to have an outlet—exercise, for example, or some sort of creative endeavor. Art, music, photography, writing: any of those would help. Better yet, learn to open up with at least one or two people!

Gemini

Rules: hands, arms, lungs, nervous system

2013 Tip:

Begin your year of transformation by focusing on one area of your life that you would like to improve, to clean up. You often tend to spread yourself too thin, so the focus will benefit you.

Health and Fitness

You benefit from periodic breaks in your established routine. Whether it's a trip to some exotic port or the grocery, it's a breath of fresh air, a way to hit the pause button on your busy mind. Regular physical exercise helps to bleed off some of your energy and keeps your already youthful body supple and in shape.

As a mutable air sign you need intellectual stimulation and a constant array of experiences and information that keep your curiosity piqued. Otherwise it's too easy for all that nervous energy to turn inward and affect your health. The kind of work you do is important in the overall scheme of your health. You do best in nonroutine kinds of work with flexible hours or preferably in a profession where you make your own hours! Any job in communication, travel, public relations would suit you. When you're passionate about what you do, you're happier. If you're happy, your immune system remains healthy.

With your natural dexterity and coordination, you would do well at yoga. If you don't take classes yet, sign up for some. Not only will it keep you flexible, but you'll benefit mentally. Meditation would also be an excellent practice for you. Anything to calm your busy head!

Since your respiratory and nervous systems are your most vulnerable areas, your diet should include plenty of fish, fresh fruits, and vegetables. If you live in a place where you can garden, plant some of these items for optimum freshness. Vitamin C, zinc, the B vitamins, and vitamins E and A are also beneficial for you. With your energy always in fast-forward, it's smart to get at least seven or preferably eight hours of sleep a night. If you're the type of Gemini with a high metabolism, then you benefit from eating several small meals throughout the day rather than just the usual three.

Cancer

Rules: breasts, stomach, digestive system

2013 Tip:

During this year of transformation step out of your subjective universe and try to see the world through someone else's eyes. Zip yourself up in another's skin.

Health and Fitness

As a cardinal water sign you benefit from proximity to water. If you can live or work close to a body of water, you'll notice a marked difference in your energy and intuition and how you feel and think. Even a vacation close to the water is healing. This seems to hold true not only for Cancer sun signs, but for moon and rising signs in Cancer too. The body of water can be anything—a lake, river, ocean, salt marsh, even a pond!

Not surprisingly, you benefit from any kind of water sport, even a day at the beach or a picnic by the river. The point is that water speaks to you. It feels like your natural element. You might want to read *The Secret of Water* or any of the other books by Masaru Emoto. You will never think of water in the same way again and will be more conscious of how human emotions affect water—and thus our bodies, since we consist of nearly 70 percent water.

Emotionally, you may cling to past injuries and hurts more than other signs or may still be dragging around issues from childhood or even from a past life. Unresolved emotional stuff can lodge in your body and create problems. So it's important that you rid yourself of past resentments and anger. Use hypnosis to dislodge these feelings. Forgive and forget. Have a past-life regression. Read Louise Hay's book, *You Can Heal Your Life*.

If you have a moon, rising, or another planet in an earth sign, consider regular workouts at a gym.

Leo

Rules: heart, back, spinal cord

2013 Tip:

For the year of transformation promise yourself there will be a minimum of drama in your personal life. Whenever you feel yourself at the brink of an emotional outburst or meltdown, detach, step back.

Health and Fitness

Leo rules the heart. So you benefit from a low-fat diet, exercise, work that you love, and relationships in which you are recognized as the unique person that you are. Yes, those last two things count in the overall picture of your health!

Let's talk about your work. Acting, of course, is what you're known for. And performance. And politics. And, well, anything where you can show off your abundant talents. So if right now you're locked into a humdrum job, low person on the bureaucratic totem pole, and don't receive the attention you feel you deserve, then your pride and ambition are suffering. That in turn creates resentment that could be eating you alive. Turn the situation around by finding a career or an outlet where your talents shine and you're appreciated and recognized. You're a natural leader whose flamboyant style and magnetism attract the supporters who can help you.

You have a temper, but once you blow, that's it. Unlike Cancer, you don't hold on to grudges or harbor resentments or anger from childhood. You tend to be forward looking in your outlook, and your natural optimism is healthy for your heart and immune system. Anything you can do to maintain your cheerful disposition is a plus. When you feel yourself getting down, rent comedies, find books that make you laugh out loud, blog about your feelings.

Virgo

Rules: intestines, abdomen, female reproductive system

2013 Tip:

Since this is the year of transformation, be as detailed and specific as possible about an exercise routine. If you go to the gym three days a week, extend it to four or five days. If you take yoga once a week, try doing it twice a week. If you meditate five minutes a day, go for ten minutes.

Health and Fitness

If you're the type of Virgo who worries and frets a lot, then the first place it's likely to show up is in your digestive tract. You might have colic as an infant, stomach upsets as a teenager, ulcers as an adult. The best way to mitigate this tendency, of course, is to learn how NOT to worry and to simply go with the flow.

You do best on a diet that includes plenty of fresh fruits and vegetables, fish, and chicken. Try to stay away from fried or heavily spiced foods. Red meat might be difficult to digest. If you live in a place where fresh fruits and vegetables are difficult to find during the winter, then supplement your diet with the appropriate vitamins and minerals. If you're a fussy eater — and some Virgos are — then the vitamin and mineral supplements are even more important.

You benefit from hot baths, massages, anything that allows you to relax into the moment. Yoga, running, swimming, gym workouts — any of these exercise regimens benefits you. Some Virgos, particularly double Virgos — with a moon or rising in that sign — have an acute sense of smell. If you're one of those, then be sure to treat yourself to scented soaps and lotions, fragrant candles and incense, and any other scent that soothes your soul.

Virgo is typically associated with service, and you may find that whenever you do a good deed for someone, when you volunteer your time or expertise, you feel better about yourself and life in general. The more you can do to trigger these feelings, the healthier you'll be. You have a tendency toward self-criticism that's part and parcel of your need for perfection, and whenever you find yourself shifting into that critical frame of mind, stop it in its tracks. Reach for a more uplifting thought. This will help you to maintain your health.

Libra

Rules: lower back, kidney, diaphragm

2013 Tip:

You're always seeking the very thing that probably eludes you: balance. So during this year of transformation, be as independent as you can. Put yourself first. Do what *you* enjoy.

Health and Fitness

If your love life is terrific, your health probably is, too. You're happiest when you're in a relationship, preferably a committed, lifetime relationship. When things between you and your partner are on an even keel, your energy is greater, your immune system works without a hitch, you sleep more soundly, and you're more apt to have a healthier lifestyle.

You prefer working in an environment that's aesthetically pleasing, where there's a minimum of drama, and with congenial people. If your work situation doesn't fit that description, it could affect your health—and for the same reasons as a love life that is lacking. Emotions. Your lower back, kidneys, and diaphragm are vulnerable areas for you, and unvented emotions could manifest in those areas first. If it isn't possible to change jobs or careers right now, then find an artistic outlet for your creative expression. Music, photography, art, writing, dance, any area that allows you to flex your creativity.

You benefit from yoga, walking, swimming, and any kind of exercise that strengthens your lower-back muscles. Meditation is also beneficial, particularly when it's combined with an awareness of breathing.

The healthiest diet for you should consist of foods with varied tastes, plenty of fresh fruits and vegetables—organic if possible—and a minimum of meats. Anything that benefits your kidneys is good. Drink at least eight glasses of water a day, so that your kidneys are continually flushed out.

Scorpio

Rules: sexual organs, elimination

2013 Tip:

In this year of transformation, a process you understand well, allow your considerable intuition to guide you in all matters, including your health.

Health and Fitness

As a fixed water sign you probably benefit by a proximity to water every bit as much as Cancer does. Lake, ocean, river, pond, salt marsh: take your pick. If none of these is available, put a fountain in your backyard or somewhere in your house and create a meditation area. It's important that you have a quiet center where you can decompress at the end of the day, particularly if you have a busy family life and a lot of demands on your time.

You tend to keep a lot of emotion locked inside, and if the emotions are negative—resentment, anger—they fester and affect your health. So try to find someone you can talk to freely about your emotions—a partner, friend, family member. Or pour these feelings into a creative outlet. One way or another, get them out.

Scorpio rules the sexual and elimination organs, so these areas could be where ill health hits first. Be sure that you eat plenty of roughage and enjoy what you eat while you're eating it. Stay away from the usual culprits—fried or heavily processed foods. You do best with plenty of fresh food but may want to consider eliminating red meats. Consider colonics treatments for cleaning out the bowels.

For your overall health it's important to enjoy sex with a partner whom you trust. Avoid using sex as a leverage for power in a relationship.

Sagittarius

Rules: hips, thighs, liver

2013 Tip:

To keep yourself really healthy in this year of transformation, attend to details—emotional, physical, intellectual, and spiritual. Be precise.

Health and Fitness

As a mutable fire sign you can't tolerate any kind of restriction or limitation on your freedom. You must be able to get up and go whenever you want. If you work in a job that demands you punch a time clock and your hours are strictly regulated, or are in a relationship where you feel constricted, then you probably aren't happy. For a naturally buoyant and happy person like you, that could spell health challenges. Sadge rules the hips, sacral region of the spine, coccygeal vertebrae, femur, ileum, iliac arteries, and sciatic nerves, so any of these areas could be impacted health-wise.

You benefit from any kind of athletic activity. From competitive sports to an exercise regimen you create, your body craves regular activity. You also benefit from yoga, which keeps your spine and hips flexible.

If you're prone to putting on weight—and even if

you're not!—strive to minimize sweets and carbs in your diet. The usual recommendations—abundant fresh vegetables and fruits—also apply. If you're the type who eats on the run, then you may be eating fast or heavily processed foods and should try to keep that at a minimum or eliminate it altogether. Even though your digestive system is hard enough to tolerate just about anything, the fast foods and processed foods add carbs and calories.

Antioxidants are beneficial, of course, and these include vitamins C, A, and E. Minerals like zinc should be included in your diet and also a glucosamine supplement for joints.

Capricorn

Rules: knees, skin, bones

2013 Tip:

During this year of transformation ease up on yourself. You tend to be quite the workaholic, and it's okay to back off for a while, to give yourself a break, dive into a creative venture for the sheer joy of it.

Health and Fitness

Since you seem to have been born with an innate sense of where you're going—or want to go—it's likely that you take care of yourself. You know the routine as well as anyone—eat right, stay fit, exercise, get enough rest. But there are other components to living long and prospering (to paraphrase Spock!), and that's your emotions.

You, like Scorpio, are secretive, although your motives are different. For you it's a privacy factor more than anything else. You keep your emotions to yourself and may not express what you feel when you feel it. This can create blockages in your body, notably in your joints or knees. It's vital that you learn to vent your emotions, to rid yourself of anger before it has a chance to move inward.

You're focused, ambitious, and patient in the attainment of your goals. But your work—your satisfaction with it—is a primary component in your health. If you feel you've reached a dead end in your career, if you're frustrated more often than you're happy with what you do, then it's time to revamp and get out of Dodge. By taking clear, definite steps toward something else, you feel you're more in control of your destiny and mitigate the possibility of health challenges.

Since your knees are vulnerable, running is probably not the best form of exercise for you, unless you do it only once or twice a week and engage in some other form of exercise the rest of the time. For a cardio workout that isn't as tough on your knees, try a rowing machine. For general flexibility, there's nothing like yoga!

Aquarius

Rules: ankles, shins, circulatory system

2013 Tip:

For this year, Aquarius, develop your intuition. Attend a workshop in intuitive development. Experiment with various divination systems. Learn to read the signs and symbols in your life.

Health and Fitness

Let's start with the effect of Uranus ruling your sign. It sometimes can set your nerves on edge—too many sounds, too much chaos around you, loud noises deep into the night, the backfiring of cars, the incessant drone of traffic, even a crowd at the local mall. You're sensitive to all of that. It's part of what makes it important for you to have a private space to which you can withdraw—a quiet backyard filled with plants, a room inside your house with an altar for your Wiccan practice, filled with scents from candles or incense that soothe your frazzled nerves. Or perhaps a book on tape can shut it all out. But shut it out you must to protect your health.

Because you live so much inside your own head, exercise is definitely beneficial for you. It doesn't have to be anything complicated—yoga done in the privacy of your own home, long walks, regular bike rides. But do *something* to ground your body, to get your blood moving, to silence the buzz inside your head. It will all benefit your health.

Nutrition? Well, for an Aquarius, this can go any number of different ways. You enjoy different types of food, so that's a place to start—with what you *enjoy*. The foods are likely to be unusual—organically grown, for instance, prepared in unusual ways, or purchased from a local co-op. If you live in the city, perhaps you purchase food from a grocery store you've been frequenting for years. The idea here is that *you* know what's best for your body, what you can tolerate, what you need. Even though Aquarians aren't generally as in touch with their bodies as earth signs, they have an intuitive sense about what works for them. In the end that's all that matters.

Pisces

Rules: the feet, is associated with the lymphatic system

2013 Tip:

Treat yourself to a weekend at a spa. Pamper yourself. In this year of transformation bestow on yourself the attention you usually shower on others.

Health and Fitness

Let's start with emotions. Let's start with the fact that you're a psychic sponge, able to absorb other people's moods and thoughts with the ease of a magnet attracting every other piece of metal around it. Yes, let's start there. It's why you should associate only with optimistic, upbeat people. The negative types steal your energy, wreck your immune system, and leave you in a tearful mess at the end of the rainbow with nothing to show for your journey.

Like your fellow water signs Cancer and Scorpio, you probably benefit from proximity to water. Whether you live near water, work near it, or vacation near it, water refreshes your soul, spirit, intuition, and your immune system. Read Masaru Emoto's books on how water responds to emotions and intent. You'll never think about water in the same way again. You'll never think about your sun sign in the same way again either.

You benefit from any kind of exercise, but try something that speaks to your soul. Swimming. Rowing, but in an actual boat, on an actual river instead of in a gym. Even a hot tub where you kick your legs is beneficial. Pay attention to the water you drink. Is your tap water filled with fluorides? Then avoid it and look for distilled water. Drink at least eight glasses a day. Indulge yourself in massages, foot reflexology, periodic dips in the ocean. Any ocean.

CHAPTER 5

You and Your Money in 2013

Right now, in early 2011, signs of the recession that started in 2007 are still painfully evident. In August 2010, for instance, nearly 15 million people remained unemployed, and the unemployment rate was just under 10 percent. In some areas of the country—Michigan, for instance—the unemployment rate is higher.

According to an article from the AP in mid-September 2010, more homes were foreclosed in August 2010 than at any point during the mortgage crisis—95,364, to be exact. RealtyTrac's figures are staggering: since 2007 more than 2.3 million homes have been foreclosed. As of September 16, 2010, CNBC reported that the states with the highest foreclosure rates were, in descending order: Hawaii, Illinois, Michigan, Georgia, Utah, Idaho, California, Arizona, Florida, and Nevada.

These figures point to a troubling pattern that has been prevalent throughout the early twenty-first century—greed. Whether it's corporate or individual greed, there are no free rides. Banks lent to people who didn't have the income to meet mortgage payments, bundled good and bad mortgages together, and sold them off. Borrowers used their homes as ATM machines. In a sense what is happening to the American economy is a reflection of what has happened to the U.S. economy overall: we are living beyond our means. Right now the U.S. debt stands at more than $13 trillion. In fact, you can check the debt, live, right here: http://www.brillig.com/debt_clock

So what do all these depressing statistics mean for you in 2013? Well, you may be taking a deeper look this year at your financial picture — and your attitudes and beliefs about money. Are you a risk-taker? Do you stash away a percentage of everything you make? Do you spend money as quickly as it comes in? Do you have a realistic budget? Are you in credit-card debt? Do you live debt free? Depending on your financial situation, here are tips for each sign on how to maximize your potential this year; when the stars favor your finances — and when they don't.

But first take this inventory about your beliefs concerning money.

Belief Inventory

Here's a list of some commonly held negative beliefs about money. Check the ones to which you subscribe:

- Money is the root of all evil.
- Money is nonspiritual.
- The rich have major problems in their lives.
- Money corrupts.

- If you have too much money, you have to worry about losing it.
- If you have too much money, it takes over your life.
- The wealthy don't have money problems, but they have a lot of other problems.

You get the idea here. Many of these beliefs we've adopted from family and peers and have held on to them because they're comfortable, we believe they're true, or because we don't even realize we believe them! So if you're not satisfied with what you're earning, start monitoring how you think about money. Any time you find yourself thinking a negative thought about money, turn the thought around by thinking something more positive. Also, read Napoleon Hills' classic *Think and Grow Rich* and *Money and the Law of Attraction* by Esther and Jerry Hicks.

Now let's take a look at how you can maximize your earning potential in 2013.

Aries

You fall into several distinct types. One type is an impulsive spender: you see something you like, whip out the plastic, and buy it. Then you suffer the next month when that bill comes due, along with all your other bills. Then there's another type of Aries, who saves for something special—a trip, an appliance, a car—but isn't saving long range. Another type saves with the distant future in mind. Which type do you fit into?

There are two excellent periods this year for finances. The first period falls between March 21 and

April 15, when Venus is in your sign. This period is excellent for earning additional money for sales, asking for a raise. The second period, when Venus transits Taurus and your financial area, falls between April 15 and May 9. During this period you may be more prone toward saving rather than spending. But if you do feel the urge to spend, it may be for high-end items—art, jewelry. So if you succumb to the urge, be sure to pay cash!

Although we talk about Jupiter transits in a later chapter, this planet's transit through Gemini could be quite nice for your finances. That time frame: January 1 to June 25. Excellent backup dates: March 12 to April 20, when Mars transits your sign.

Taurus

As a fixed earth sign you're more the saving than the spending type. That said, you enjoy your creature comforts and can be easily seduced by big-ticket items—art, jewelry, that top-of-the-line mountain bike, a yoga retreat in Costa Rica. One thing you enjoy is good food. Your palate is well developed, and there isn't much that you won't eat. But food is really special when it's exotic, so one of your main expenses may be restaurants!

An excellent time this year for maximizing your earning potential falls between April 15 and May 9, when Venus is in your sign. This period is one in which you feel extremely good about yourself and life in general, and that feeling bolsters your self-confidence. Others pick up on this, and suddenly, Taurus, you can do no wrong. You get hired for that job you want, you land a promotion or raise, you sell your novel.

The next period that could pay off financially falls between June 25, 2013, and July 16, 2014, when Jupiter transits Cancer, a water sign compatible with your earth-sign sun. This occurs in your solar third house of communication and travel. Perhaps this would be a good time to dust off that old manuscript. Or perhaps there's a new gold mine awaiting you in travel!

Good backup dates: April 20 to May 31, when Mars transits your sign. This one kicks butt, Taurus.

Gemini

Left to your own devices, you think things like checkbooks and saving accounts, IRAs and investments, are for other people to ponder—like your accountant, partner, parents, sibling. You would rather write and talk about *ideas*. So let's talk about the *idea* of money. What does it actually represent to you? Energy? Freedom? Albatross? During this year of transformation it's to your advantage to look at money as energy and freedom. The more you make, the greater your freedom to do what interests you. The more effort you expend, the greater the energy you're putting into what you do and the greater the return. At least that's how it's supposed to work in theory. But you have to remain focused, resolute.

One of your best times this year for increasing your earnings falls between January 1 and June 25, when expansive Jupiter transits your sign. This transit has been going on since 2012, so by now you should have a clear idea how it works and the kind of luck and expansion that accompanies it. Another excellent period for increasing your earnings occurs between May

9 and June 2, when Venus transits your sign and travels with Jupiter. Things may seem to be going so well that you could be tempted to kick back and chill. Resist that temptation! Use this time frame to move forward—ask for a raise, apply for a promotion, look for a new job that pays more.

Another favorable financial period occurs between May 9 and June 2, when Venus transits your sign. This transit should be good for you financially and otherwise. You have such appeal now that it's easy for you to get the job you apply for or land that raise, that promotion, that big sale. Believe it—and watch it happen.

An excellent backup period is May 31 to July 13, when Mars transits your sign. It propels you toward what you desire.

Cancer

You probably do well budgeting your money. In fact you probably know exactly what you earn, what you spend, and on what. You're not obsessed with money, but you recognize that you spend at least forty hours a week earning your living, so it makes sense to keep track of your finances. You tend to be a saver, not just for the short term but for the long term as well.

This year there are several periods that favor your finances. The first occurs between June 2 and 27, when Venus transits your sign. During this period ask for a raise or promotion, apply for new jobs, network with professional peers, open an IRA. Keep in mind, though, that Mercury is retrograde in your sign between June 26 and July 20, so just to be safe confine the above suggestions to June 2 to 25!

The second period when your finances—and just about everything else in your life—may undergo radical expansion occurs between June 25, 2013, and July 16, 2014. Jupiter transits your sign during this period, and what a treat it should be for you, Cancer. You'll feel as if you're in the right place at the right time, that the sky is literally the limit. An excellent backup period occurs between July 13 and August 27, when Mars is in your sign. This transit acts like a booster rocket, and it shouts, *Go for it!*

Leo

Your flamboyance and flair for drama probably translate into expenses for clothing, home furnishings, cars, jewelry, and anything else that catches your eye. It's not that you're constantly on the prowl for these expensive items, simply that when you spend money, this is where it goes. If you make a great deal of money, then it's not a problem. But if you're supporting a family, have a child in college, a mortgage, or a middle-class income, it could be a challenge.

Your first step, then, is inventory. Take a look at how much you make and deduct the taxes and FICA that you pay and anything else that is deducted automatically from your pay. That figure is what you actually earn in hard cash. Now take a look at your monthly expenses. How much money is left over after you pay those expenses?

There are some good times in 2013 for increasing your earnings. The first period falls between June 27 and July 22, when Venus transits your sign. This one really boosts self-confidence, other people find you infinitely appealing, and you can do no wrong, Leo. So ask for a raise or promotion, send out résumés. Unexpected bonuses or royalties could arrive during this time. If so, stash the money in an IRA.

The next period falls between January 1 and June 25, when Jupiter transits compatible air sign Gemini. Luck and expansion, Leo! This can be applied to any area of your life.

Virgo

You're the most discriminating of signs, measured, deliberate, with a penchant for details. You can be something of a perfectionist too, but rarely demand of others what you demand of yourself. Whatever you take on, you do so with complete dedication. So in 2013 perfect your finances, Virgo. Set your monetary goal, then figure out how best to achieve it.

One of the most favorable periods for earning more falls between July 22 and August 16, when Venus transits your sign. This period is favorable for landing a raise or promotion, receiving money from unexpected sources—an insurance payment, a royalty check—and sending out résumés for a job that pays you more. It's good for pitching manuscripts and screenplays.

Another potentially profitable period occurs between June 25, 2013, and July 16, 2014, when Jupiter transits compatible water sign Cancer and forms a beneficial angle to your sun. This period is when you're in the right place at the right time to bolster your bank account, land a raise, or make money by expanding your services or products to overseas markets.

Excellent backup dates: October 15 to December 7,

when Mars is in your sign. Think of this transit as your booster rocket.

Libra

Like Taurus, the other Venus-ruled sign, you enjoy being surrounded by beauty. Chances are that some of your disposable income goes toward art, jewelry, flowers, beautiful furniture—like a piano?—or perhaps toward some idiosyncratic collection you have. You can certainly save when you want to, though, and in this year of transformation it's smart to have a buffer.

Even if you earn more money this year, Libra, and you probably will, stash away a fixed percentage. Put it in an IRA or savings account, or simply take the cash and hide it somewhere! Between August 16 and September 11 Venus, your ruler, transits your sign. This period should be particularly good for you. Venus is happy in your sign and can help you to bring in additional income from a variety of different sources. If you're in sales, then you can sell anything to anyone. You might sell a manuscript, piece of art, or some other product born of your creativity.

During Jupiter's transit of fellow air sign Gemini between January 1 and June 25 you may experience an expansion in your income that seems to happen without any effort on your part. That's an illusion, of course. You have been seeding the possibilities for quite a while now. Excellent backup dates: December 7 to July 26, when Mars is in your sign. This long transit is due to a retrograde between March 1 and May 20, 2014. But while Mars is moving direct, it's your best friend, your booster rocket!

Scorpio

You're no stranger to transformation. With Pluto as the ruler of your sign, your life is constantly undergoing transformation of some kind. But if you would like to transform your finances, then 2013 is the year for you to seize the reins, Scorpio, and make things happen. Your considerable intuition and ability to get to the absolute bottom line of anything you research and investigate serve you well this year.

Between September 11 and October 7 Venus transits your sign. So during this period ask for a raise, apply for a promotion, send out résumés for jobs that really interest you. Be proactive. You and your ideas appeal to others. Another excellent period for expanding your income occurs between June 25, 2013, and July 16, 2014, when Jupiter transits fellow water sign Cancer and forms a beneficial angle to your sun. This period should be productive for you, with new creative opportunities that could bring in additional income.

Saturn begins the year in your sign, Scorpio, which could cause some delays or restrictions in your life. It's important that you meet your responsibilities and obligations so that Saturn's energies work to create solid financial foundations for you.

Sagittarius

Let the good times roll ... and roll! As a mutable fire sign your life is about activity and forward motion. You don't have time for things like budgets, balancing a checkbook, keeping track of what you earn and spend. Then when it's time to do your taxes, you freak out. You can't find receipts, your files are messed up—you get the idea. So this year, Sadge, make organization of your finances one of your priorities. Once you've done that, you can receive the full benefit of several opportune times for increasing your income. More money means more travel, and if you're like most Sadges, travel feeds your nomadic soul.

Between October 7 and November 5 Venus transits your sign. Not only does your self-confidence soar, but others find you appealing and want you on their team. So ask for a raise or promotion, pitch your ideas, submit your manuscript or screenplay or some other product you have created.

Between January 1 and June 25 Jupiter transits Gemini, your opposite sign. During this period your professional partnerships expand, and that expansion could be a big boost to you financially.

Capricorn

As a cardinal earth sign you build your financial world just as you do everything else—one brick at a time. You do it patiently and methodically and usually have a goal in mind—double your earnings in six months, for instance. Or pay off your mortgage in the next two years.

In 2013 you have several windows of opportunity when it's easier to increase your earnings, launch a business, pitch an idea that someone will buy, sell a book. Luck is on your side, you're in the right place at the right time, you meet exactly the right people who make things happen. The first period falls between January 9 and February 1, when Venus is in your sign.

This transit is a confidence booster. When you feel good about yourself, others pick up on it, and suddenly everything flows your way. If you're looking for a better-paying job or a second job, then this period could bring news.

The second period occurs between June 25, 2013, and July 16, 2014, when Jupiter transits your opposite sign, Cancer. This transit should expand your professional partnerships, which in turn could be very positive for your finances.

You have an additional plus this year. Saturn is in Scorpio, forming a strong and beneficial angle to your sun. This transit helps you to build solid financial foundations.

Aquarius

You don't really fit into any financial category. Some Aquarius are great with money, others aren't. Some are savers, others are spenders. But one thing is for sure. When you make up your mind to do something, you do it. No one and nothing can sway you from a path you've chosen. So in this year of transformation let's look at times when your income can increase.

One of the most favorable periods falls between February 1 and 25. Venus transits your sign, so your appeal is broad, and others like you and your ideas, making this an ideal time to ask for a raise. Ask with the expectation that the raise will be given. Whether you're sending out résumés or interviewing for jobs, you're in your element and should reap the rewards you so justly deserve.

Another good period for you falls between January

1 and June 25, when Jupiter transits fellow air sign Gemini. This transit has been going on since 2012, so you probably have noticed the kinds of gifts it can bring. Follow the signs and synchronicities, Aquarius. During this period you're in the right place at the right time.

Pisces

Your considerable imagination and intuition will prove enormously valuable in this year of transformation. Whatever you can imagine, after all, can manifest itself. So if you're imagining a quantum leap in your income, Pisces, fix a figure firmly in mind, focus on it, release it—and let the universe figure out the connections that must be made for you to earn that amount of money.

In the interim, of course, it's smart not to just sit back, but to become more proactive. If you dislike your job, then figure out what you would like to be doing and start submitting applications and résumés. If you often find yourself short of money, set up a realistic budget and try to stick to it. You know, do the small stuff!

Timing is essential, so let's take a look at the windows of opportunity in 2013 when things really flow your way. These periods are when you should ask for a raise or promotion, submit résumés, schedule interviews, do whatever you can to earn more. The first period falls between February 25 and March 21, when Venus transits your sign. This is when you're more you than ever! Turn on the charm; let your muse in 24/7. The second period is lengthy—June 25, 2013, to July 16, 2014. Jupiter transits fellow water sign Cancer and forms a beneficial angle to your sun. Expansion, luck, you're in the right place at the right time!

CHAPTER 6

Career Choices in 2013

At the pinnacle of the Great Depression in 1933 almost 25 percent of the nation's work force — nearly 13 million people — was unemployed. As of late October 2011 unemployment in the U.S. hovered just under 10 percent, with nearly 15 million people unemployed. Lower percentage, but more people. However, in the Great Depression, the social safety nets were missing — unemployment insurance, Social Security, Medicare, Medicaid, food stamps, and other welfare programs. Also, thanks to technological advances, the variety of available jobs is broader than it was in the 1930s.

So despite all the grim statistics, many people flourish financially during difficult times. How can you be one of them? If you've been laid off from your job, the first thing you can do to turn things around is to look at it as an opportunity. Take stock of your talents and passions. What would you most enjoy doing? Is there a way you can turn your passions into a moneymaker?

Maybe you've always wanted to work with animals

in some capacity. If so, volunteer at your local animal shelter or at a private animal rescue center. With a little luck, determination, and focus, you might be able to turn it into a full-time job. Or, if you were going to start a business, what sort of business would it be? Do your market research and determine if there's a niche that your service or talent could fill.

The more positive and upbeat your attitude, the more frequently you view every challenge as an opportunity, the greater the chances that you'll turn things around.

Several years ago friends of ours, a married couple who are both writers, had pretty much hit rock bottom. The wife admitted that she was ready to start cleaning pools just to have a steady income. Then practically overnight everything turned around. Her husband sold a novel that became a popular cable-TV show; a producer commissioned her to write a script. Suddenly their bank account fattened, they bought a second home, new car, and boat, and the world opened up for them. It can open up for you too.

We create our realities from the inside out. Everything you see around you is a manifestation of a belief that you hold. Some of our beliefs have been passed down to us by well-meaning family members, mentors, teachers, or friends, and we adopt those beliefs because we respect the people who handed them to us. But what do *you* believe about your abilities and talents and your ability to earn your living doing what you love? How do you handle stress? Change?

In 2013 when so much of the world seems to be shifting beneath our feet, we have a chance to delve into those beliefs and get rid of the ones we have adopted out of convenience. We can either go with the flow, change with the times, or offer up resistance. The more we resist, the more pain we experience. The more we go with the flow, the greater our capacity to discover where we should be. Which path will you take?

Inventory

One way to prosper professionally during good *and* bad times is to know what you want. So let's take an inventory.

1. What is your dream job/profession? Describe it. Be detailed.

   _____

   _____

   _____

2. How can you attain this dream job/profession? Do you need more education, time, additional skills? If so, include those things, and set a goal for attaining them.

   _____

   _____

   _____

3. Set realistic professional goals. Choose a time frame—a month, six months, a year, whatever feels right to you. Ask yourself what you would like to

be doing a year from now. Describe it in detail. Make it real!

_____

_____

_____

4. Inner work is just as important as the external steps you take to realize a goal. You might, for example, start meditating as a way to ground yourself and mitigate any stress you're experiencing. Or perhaps you start using visualization daily to help you to achieve your goal. You may work to deepen your intuition and to create more positive beliefs. Describe in detail your plan for inner work.

_____

_____

_____

5. What are your greatest strengths? Describe them. Then focus on the strengths you have, not your weaknesses.

_____

_____

_____

Using Synchronicity in 2013

The Swiss psychologist Carl Jung coined the term. It means the coming together of inner and outer events in a way that can't be explained by cause and effect and that is meaningful to the observer. Or, it's a meaningful coincidence. When it happens to you, don't dismiss it as a random curiosity. A synchronicity can be a navigational tool, a confirmation, warning, or guidance.

For Frank Morgan, an actor who played five different parts in *The Wizard of Oz*, a stunning synchronicity served as confirmation that he was on the right professional track by accepting parts in the movie.

One of the parts he played was the disreputable Professor Marvel. For that role the director and wardrobe man wanted him dressed in a "nice-looking coat, but tattered," said Mary Mayer, a unit publicist on the film. So they traipsed down to a second-hand clothing store and purchased a rack of coats. Then Frank, the director, and the wardrobe guy all got together and selected one of the coats.

Imagine his surprise when he turned a pocket of the coat inside out and found a name sewn into the lining: L. Frank Baum, the author of *The Wizard of Oz*. The additional synchronicity here is that both men who wore the coat were named Frank.

One of the most common types of synchronicities involves clusters of numbers, names, objects, words, songs, events. Jung experienced many kinds of clusters throughout this life. He believed that numbers are "an archetype of order which has become conscious." So if you begin to experience clusters while you're reinventing your professional life, pay close attention. If the cluster involves a name or the title of a book or song, then it may hold a vital clue about the direction you're taking professionally. If the cluster involves a number, then research its esoteric meaning.

In the past few years hundreds of thousands of people have begun experiencing clusters of 11, 111, and 11:11. Famed Israeli psychic Uri Geller devotes an extensive section of his Web site to 11:11. Several books have been written about it. If you Google 11:11, nearly 200 million links come up. Some of the esoteric meanings: you're on the right track, in the right place at the right time, are being ushered into a greater awareness. So if you begin to notice this particular cluster in your life, know you're headed in exactly the right direction!

While writing this section, we took a break to check the counter on our blog for today and laughed! It was 111.

In times of stress or major transitions—marriage, divorce, birth, a move, career change, or change in employment and income—synchronicities may occur more frequently. Decipher the message if you can, and know that synchronicities indicate we're in the flow, exactly where we're supposed to be.

Your Career Path in 2013

Regardless of what you do for a living, whether you love or detest it or merely tolerate it, you can maximize your strengths and talents to enhance your professional opportunities.

Aries

Ah, Aries. You're restless and impatient. Nothing happens quickly enough for you. As a cardinal fire sign this is to be expected. Your entire life is about movement, action, doing. You're the pioneer, the entrepreneur, the one who really does march to the beat of a different drummer. Your pioneering spirit is your most valuable asset for navigating any professional changes you encounter this year.

Whenever you encounter a challenge or block, you just slam your way through it, leaving a trail of debris in your wake. It might be to your advantage to assess the situation first, then find a gentler means of moving through the block. Usually the word *defeat* doesn't exist in your vocabulary. What someone else might see as a setback, you view as an opportunity.

In 2011 you learned to follow your passions, wherever they led; in 2012 that faith began to pay off; in 2013 the transformation in your professional life should be underway.

Taurus

Few signs are as sensuous and grounded as you are, Taurus. As a fixed earth sign you know your own mind and what you want. Your senses are finely attuned to your environment, you hear the music of the spheres, poetry flows through your dreams, you have the heart and soul of a mystic. You're the most enduring, taciturn, and physical of the twelve signs. You always finish what you start unless it's just unbearable!

In 2011 you learned that your resolute determination is your greatest asset for navigating professional changes. In 2012 you learned to trust your intuition. In 2013 your hard work begins to pay off. Until June 25 of this year expansive Jupiter will be in your financial area, so that's where the payoff begins. Your income should soar. Whether this increase comes from a traditional nine-to-five job or from your own business is irrelevant as long as you're enjoying what you do.

You already know your own value. In 2012 the people around you learned it, and in 2013 they are fully in your court.

Gemini

Your curiosity and ability to communicate with just about anyone anywhere are your greatest assets in 2013. As a mutable air sign flexibility and adapting to change are a snap for you. Your mind is such a hive of activity, buzzing constantly with information, that you just have to get it out somehow, some way. So perhaps 2013 is your time to start a blog or build a Web site, and figure out how to make money from it.

Do you have a particular service to sell? An area of expertise? Have you always wanted to write a book or screenplay? Then as the saying goes, Gemini, there's no time like the present. With 2013 as the year of transformation, it's your turn to shine. In fact until June 25 expansive Jupiter will be in your sign. So plant your seeds during this time, Gemini. Take chances. Expand your horizons. In 2011 you learned to follow the impulses of your curiosity to see where they might lead, and they led some mighty strange places. But you were in the right place at the right time. In 2012 your versatility and communication abilities enabled you to navigate the paradigm shift that's underway. In 2013 you're able to put everything you've learned into action.

Cancer

You're completely attuned to emotions—yours and everyone else's. It's easy for you to slip into someone else's skin and feel what they feel. You hurt as they hurt. You weep as they weep. You laugh as they laugh. Like fellow water sign Pisces you're a psychic sponge, an empath. Your extraordinary memory is intimately linked to your emotions, and your intuition is remarkable. All of these traits helped you to successfully navigate the transitions of 2011. During the first six months of 2012, when Jupiter was in compatible earth sign Taurus, your hard work really began to pay off. You met people who not only shared your interests but who were helpful in some way professionally. Your professional options expanded. Perhaps you launched a business, wrote a novel, had a photography exhibit. One way or another you began to achieve your dreams.

In 2013 you have opportunities to use what you've learned these last two years and put your prodigious intuition to work for you. The period to watch for: June 25, 2013, to mid-July 2014.

Leo

You were born to express your creativity through performance. You love the applause, the recognition, the immediate gratification and feedback. Of course, not every Leo is an actor or actress, but every Leo loves drama. So whether you're on the stage, in front of a classroom, or counseling a patient in therapy, your creative flair moves through you like a force of nature.

In 2011 you learned how valuable this asset was in

helping you to navigate any professional changes you experienced. In 2012 you were well positioned for the unfolding of your dreams. Between January 1 and June 25, 2013, when Jupiter is in compatible air sign Gemini, everything expands for you—opportunity, finances, your personal relationships, your career.

Virgo

Your gift is details. Whether it's your own life that you're honing, sculpting, and shining like some fine gem or a particular project or relationship, you can see the finished product in a way that others can't. You also have a particular gift or ability that you're always willing to provide to others, without thought of compensation. These traits carried you through professional changes you may have experienced in 2011.

The first six months of 2012, when Jupiter was in fellow earth sign Taurus, were probably magnificent for you. Your worldview expanded, you may have traveled extensively overseas, or perhaps a publishing opportunity presented itself. But in 2013, when Jupiter transits your career area, you learn the meaning of professional bliss! The time frame to anticipate: January 1 to June 25, 2013. Prepare yourself for a wild, wonderful career ride.

Libra

You can work a room like a seasoned politician, spreading peace and harmony even among people who can't agree on anything. That's your magic. Yet the very qualities that you can instill in others often elude you. Not that any of us could tell by looking at you. Libra is a master of social camouflage. It seems that nothing ruffles you. But within you're struggling to maintain harmony without compromising your principles. Your sphere is relationships. More than any other sign, you can see the many sides of an issue and understand that your truth may not be everyone's truth. But you can live with the paradox. It's your gift.

Any professional challenges you encountered in 2011 were undoubtedly overcome by your ability to connect with people. In 2012 your professional opportunities proliferated, with enhanced creativity and new travel opportunities tossed in for good measure. In 2013 you're positioned to put it all into action.

Scorpio

You're the emotional vortex of the zodiac, a spinning whirlwind of contradictions. You aren't like the rest of us, and that's the way you prefer it. You dig deeply into everything you do, looking for the absolute bottom line, the most fundamental truth, and then you excavate everything at the discovery site just to make sure you've gotten it all.

Professional challenges that you encountered in 2011 were met with the fortitude and resilience for which you're known. In 2012 you may have launched a business or creative endeavor. In 2013, particularly between June 25, 2013, and mid-July 2014, you may find yourself traveling internationally for business, writing a book or novel, or perhaps heading off for graduate school. Your intuition is finely honed for this period; listen to it.

Sagittarius

You're the life of the party, just like your fellow fire sign Leo. But your approaches are different. Where Leo seeks recognition and applause, you're after the big picture. It doesn't matter how far you have to travel to find it, how many people you have to talk to, how many books or blogs you must read. When your passion is seized, you're as doggedly relentless as Taurus. One part of you operates from raw instinct; the other part is acculturated, aware of how to work the system.

In 2011, the year of transition, you realized that you don't recognize professional challenges. You learned that any bump in a road simply means you take an alternate path to get to where you want to go. In 2012 you may have teamed up with a partner for some entrepreneurial venture or perhaps to launch a business. In 2013 everything comes together in just the way you envisioned. But you may be tempted to take on too much responsibility, so be sure to make specific goals and proceed at a measured, realistic pace.

Capricorn

You're the achiever, the builder, the classic type-A personality whose focus is so tight that everything and everyone becomes part of your journey toward ... well, the top of the hill, the pinnacle of whatever you're attempting to reach. You can build anything, anywhere. A fictional world, belief system, invention, concept, family, video world. Name it, and you can build it.

Any professional challenges you encountered in 2011 were undoubtedly tackled the same way that you have tackled any other challenge in your life—by finding a way around it. Or through it. As a cardinal earth sign you value what is tangible, practical, and efficient, and your journey through any obstacle reflects it. In 2011 you learned how not to fear, and that got you through every professional challenge you encountered. In 2012, when Jupiter was in fellow earth sign Taurus, your muse was so up close and personal that your creativity soared. In 2013, particularly between June 25, 2013, and mid-July 2014, build strong professional partnerships. Learn to delegate.

Aquarius

You're not easy to pigeonhole. Sometimes you seem to be the paragon of independence. Yet you enjoy the company of groups who share your passions. You're the one who thinks so far outside the box that people close to you may accuse you of communication with aliens, ghosts, goblins, elves. Even if it's true, you just laugh and continue on your journey into the strange, the unknown, the heart of the universe.

Any challenges you encountered professionally in 2011 were no major thing for you. You always managed to work your way around the challenge by continuing to explore what interests you. In 2012 your creativity soared and became your most valuable asset for navigating the paradigm shift. In 2013, particularly between January 1 and June 25, when Jupiter is in fellow air sign Gemini, you're on a roll, Aquarius. Whatever you can imagine will manifest itself.

Pisces

Dreamer, healer, mystic: all these adjectives fit you, Pisces. You live within a rich, inner world that is both a buffer and a conduit to deeper experiences. You don't need anyone else to tell you this. At some level you already know it, appreciate it, embrace it. While it's true that you're a sucker for a sob story, an attribute that can turn you from hero to martyr in the space of a single breath, there's no concrete evidence that you're more of a victim than any other sun sign.

Any professional challenges that came your way during 2011 were met with your powerful intuition, prodigious imagination, and unique way of dealing with adversity through faith in your role in the larger scheme of things. The tentacles of your psychic abilities were active 24/7, at your disposal, and awaited your instructions. In 2012 you used your communication abilities to pull ahead of the competition. In 2013 your imagination and intuitive ability get you exactly where you want to be. The time frame to anticipate: June 25, 2013, to mid-July 2014.

CHAPTER 7

Aspects

In astrology we look at where transiting planets fall in the houses of our natal chart and what angles these transiting planets make to our natal planets. These angles are called aspects. For the purpose of this book we primarily look at where these transiting planets hit your solar houses and the angles they make to your sun and to each other. Some of these angles are beneficial, others are challenging.

Think of aspects as a symbolic network of arteries and veins that transport the blood of astrology. In a natal chart these angles connect our inner and outer worlds, accentuate certain traits and play down others. Each aspect represents a certain type of energy, so there really aren't any good or bad aspects because energy is neutral. It's what we do with the energy that counts. It comes back to free will. When transiting planets make angles to each other, energy is also exchanged.

For instance, every year there is at least one very lucky day when the transiting sun and transiting Jupiter form a beneficial angle to each other—a conjunction (same sign and degree), a sextile (60 degrees apart), or a trine (120 degrees apart). The lucky day in 2013 falls on June 18–19, when the sun and Jupiter are within a degree of each other or exactly conjunct. This means that the sun's life energy and Jupiter's expansive energy combine and create, well, some magic for all of us! It's especially good for Taurus and other earth signs, but since we all have Taurus somewhere in our charts, everyone benefits.

If you look back to the presidential election in November 2008, Saturn in Virgo and Uranus in Pisces formed an exact opposition to each other. They were 180 degrees apart, an aspect that is like a tug-of-war. In this case the tug-of-war was between the candidate that represented the old paradigm, the established order—Saturn—and the candidate who symbolized sweeping change—Uranus.

Aspects are most powerful as they are approaching exactness. So even though a conjunction, for example, is 00 degrees of separation or a square is technically 90 degrees of separation, many astrologers use *orbs* that can be as wide as 5 or 10 degrees. Some astrologers use small orbs, but others assign larger orbs for the sun and moon and smaller orbs for other planets. The closer the orb, the more powerful the combination. If you're sensitive to transits, then, you may be feeling lucky for several days before and after June 18–19.

In terms of a natal chart, any transiting planet that is approaching an aspect with one of your natal planets is also most powerful on its approach. The traditional aspects have been used since the second century A.D. They are the conjunction, sextile, square, trine, and opposition. These aspects are considered to be the major or hard angles and are also the most power-ful. There are other minor aspects that astrologers use, but for the purpose of this chapter, we'll only talk about the traditional aspects.

At the end of this chapter is a chart for a young man. We'll be referring to this chart as we discuss the aspects.

Conjunction, major hard aspect, 0 degrees

This aspect is easy to identify—clusters of planets within a few degrees of each other, usually but not always in the same sign and house. But it's a complex aspect because energies combine, fuse, merge. Think of it as power and intensity, and that's true whether it's in your natal chart or is a transiting planet con-juncting your sun sign. If you have conjunctions in your natal chart, the astrologer who reads for you should address what it means and how you can use it to maximize your potential.

Take a look at the young man's chart at the end of the chapter. His fourth and fifth houses are jammed with planets, with just one planet—Mercury—in his third house and just the moon and the South Node in the sixth house. His focus in this lifetime is on creativ-ity and his domestic life. With Uranus, Mars, and Nep-tune (♅,♂,♆) all in the fifth house, in Sagittarius, this young man's creative interests may involve television or radio (ruled by Uranus). He will pour plenty of energy into his creativity (Mars) and will draw on the resources of his higher self (Neptune) to achieve his creative goals. His Mars and Neptune are exactly con-junct—both at 24 degrees. This aspect is exceptionally powerful, and in self-aware people it unites physical and spiritual energy. He won't have any trouble manifesting his desires and will always attract the people and situations he needs, when he needs them.

Now look at his fourth house. Saturn, Pluto, Venus, the sun, and Jupiter are all crowded in there, with three planets in Libra and two in Scorpio. These planets suggest that his early childhood provided him with a solid foundation from which to live. There may have been some financial deprivation in his early life or excessive rules (Saturn ♄), but there was also enormous power in his family unit that enabled him to discover what made him feel secure and empowered. Venus in Libra suggests that he finds/found great pleasure in his early childhood family life and later as an adult.

With Saturn closely conjunct to both Pluto and Venus, his ambitions find concrete expression through hard work and patience. Romantic relationships are serious business for him. Once his heart is won, his loyalty is unwavering.

Sextile, major soft aspect, 60 degrees

Again, look at the young man's chart. An example of a sextile occurs between his Saturn in Libra at 25 degrees and his Mars and Neptune at 24 degrees Sagittarius. A sextile is a point of ease. It represents a free-flowing energy between the planets involved. No tension. The sextile is a kind of buffer, a shield against turmoil, indecision, instability. But if there are too many sextiles, then the person may be too passive! Again, this definition applies to sextiles within a natal chart as well as transiting sextiles to your sun sign.

The Saturn/Mars sextile suggests that he's a relentless worker, particularly when it comes to the pursuit of his wishes and dreams. He's able to channel his creative drive to achieve whatever he wants. The Saturn/Neptune sextile suggests that the dreamy, spiritual aspects of Neptune are brought down to earth. He believes that every species lives to realize its fullest potential.

There's a 3 degree sextile between Pluto and Venus in Libra and Mars and Neptune in Sagittarius. The Venus/Mars sextile indicates that he gets along well with the opposite sex. His romantic relationships are generally harmonious. Again, the creative aspect in his chart is emphasized. The Pluto/Mars sextile indicates a powerful will and determination. In self-aware individuals there's great metaphysical knowledge and wisdom that can be used to benefit humanity.

Square, major hard aspect, 90 degrees

Friction, angst, *oh my God, the sky is falling*: that's how squares feel in a natal chart. The sky, of course, is never falling, but the friction and angst are quite real and act as triggers for action, forward thrust. They force us to develop, evolve, and reach aggressively for our desires.

In the young man's chart his Capricorn moon in the sixth house (☽ ♑21) is square to his Saturn in the fourth house (♄ ♎25). This aspect can be difficult. In fact, many astrologers view it unfavorably. But famed astrologer Grant Lewi called it "the most powerful single aspect you can have in a horoscope. It gives both ambition and the ability to concentrate on it."

This young man, by the way, is now a successful videographer and filmmaker, a business he has built from the bottom up, on his own hard work and focus.

His Mercury in the third house ($\mathbf{\rlap{\,/}\rotatebox{20}{\char"263F}}{\approx}14$) forms a wide square to his Capricorn moon. Generally this square indicates a conflict between head and heart. His emotions tell him one thing, his head screams another. It's likely that the young man has a magnetic wit, can talk to anyone about anything, and has a great sense of humor.

Trines, major soft aspect, 120 degrees

This aspect works like a sextile, linking energies in a harmonious way. It's associated with general ease and good fortune, and it's the same whether it's in the natal chart or by transit.

Look at the chart again. The only trine this young man has occurs between his Mars in Sagittarius and his Midheaven—the cusp of his tenth house. This trine enables him to achieve whatever he desires professionally, and he's willing to work hard for it. He may travel internationally too, in some professional capacity. Mars rules Aries, so it rules his Midheaven—a major plus.

Opposition, major hard aspect, 180 degrees

This aspect feels like a persistent itch that you can't reach and usually involves polarities—Taurus/Scorpio, for example, or Aries/Libra. It brings about change through conflict and sometimes represents traits we project onto others because we haven't fully integrated them into ourselves. Again, the opposition applies to transits as well as to natal planets.

Due to the way the planets are clumped in this man's chart, the only opposition he has is between Mercury in Libra and his Midheaven in Aries. This man will be happiest and most productive when he's self-employed. His ideas might conflict with those of any boss. His ingenuity is abundant, and one way or another he gets his ideas across.

When planets transit this man's empty houses, particularly the houses that are directly opposite those in which the majority of his natal planets fall, he's apt to feel it strongly. This year, for instance, Uranus in Aries will be approaching an opposition with his natal Mercury. But because of Uranus' retrograde motion, the opposition won't be exact until 2014. During its approach to that exactness his daily life will pick up speed, new and exciting opportunities will infuse his awareness, and he may travel abroad on the spur of the moment. His communication abilities will be razor sharp. He may feel restless, have many brilliant and cutting edge ideas, and could be casting around for a way to express all of it.

In late summer 2015 Uranus will be approaching its opposition to his natal Saturn, Pluto, and Venus, which are all in the late degrees of Libra. Since Uranus takes seven years to transit a sign, these oppositions won't be exact until late spring and early summer of 2017.

Some other minor aspects that astrologers use are:

- the semi-square, 45 degrees. It creates irritation and friction between the planets involved.
- the septile, 51 degrees. Indicative of harmony and union in a nontraditional way. Can suggest spiritual power.
- the quincunx or inconjunct, 150 degrees separation. Indicates a need for adjustment in attitude and beliefs.

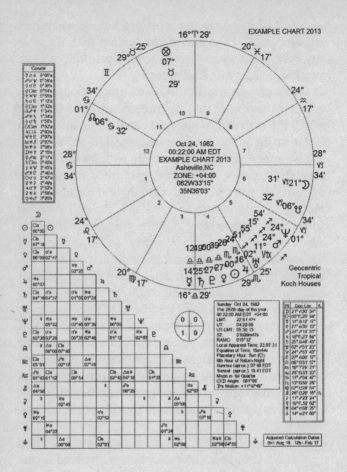

EXAMPLE CHART 2013

Oct 24, 1982
00:22:00 AM EDT
EXAMPLE CHART 2013
Asheville, NC
ZONE: +04:00
082W33'15"
35N36'03"

Geocentric
Tropical
Koch Houses

Sunday Oct 24, 1982
The 297th day of the year.
00:22:00 AM EDT +04:00
LMT: 22:51:47<
UT: 04:22:00
UT-LMT: 05:30:13
ST: 01h00m47s
RAMC: 015°12'
Local Apparent Time: 22:07:31
Equation of Time: 15m44s
Planetary Hour: Sun (☉)
6th Hour of Saturn-Night
Sunrise (approx.) 07:48 EDT
Sunset (approx.) 18:41 EDT
Moon in 1st Quarter
☉)'s Angle: 081°06'
)'s Motion: +11°47'48"

Adjusted Calculation Dates
☋: Aug 18 12h - Feb 17

106

CHAPTER 8

Moon Days

Collective Concepts of the Moon

Throughout the millennia, the moon has been the stuff of myths and fairy tales, poetry and legends. It has been worshipped and cursed and endowed with magical and curative powers. Religions have grown up around it. Sacrifices have been made to it.

In the early fifties the moon was a favorite theme in science fiction books and movies, and the storylines rarely varied: the aliens came from the moon, we colonized the moon, or the moon fell out of orbit ... you get the general picture. Even Disney issued movies in which the moon played a vital role. In one film, a Western, a woman who wore a hoop skirt typical of the American west started bouncing and kept bouncing higher and higher until she bounced right into the moon. The shadow you see in the moon is, according to Disney, that woman in the hoop skirt.

In 1969 Neil Armstrong took one giant step for mankind, and our concept of the moon was forever changed. Even though its relative position in the sky hadn't changed, everything else about it had.

We now had some idea what it really looked like, and the news was far from good. Dust, dust, and more dust. A black vacuum. Unimaginable cold. Nothingness. What's most vivid in our minds, though, is how the Earth looked from the moon—a swirling turquoise gem, a blue pearl turning in space. Our planet literally looked alive.

This was the year when Vietnam was in full swing. Americans arrived home in body bags, riots swept across college campuses, LSD was the drug of choice. People were tuning in and dropping out faster than the pictures of the moon were beamed back to Earth.

This was the year that half a million people converged on the tiny town of Woodstock, New York, to hear Hendrix, Baez, Dylan, Joplin, and all the other musicians who had captured the emotional reality of war and chaos. Women threw off their shackles. Carlos Castaneda and Aldous Huxley hurled open the doors to other realities. Camelot was dead, Martin Luther King was dead, and we had walked on the moon.

In many ways those steps of Armstrong's signaled that we were ready to confront our unconscious selves, our feminine, intuitive selves.

Fast-forward to the summer of 1997, July 4 to be exact. In the opening scenes of the movie *Independence Day*, a mammoth shadow falls across the surface of the moon. A moving shadow whose shape is unmistakable. The message comes through loud and clear: the shadow is that of a spaceship that uses the moon as a base, and now that ship is on the move toward Earth. What ensues is pure Hollywood, with Will Smith holding the record for aliens annihilated. But *Independence Day*, like Armstrong's giant step, is part of our contemporary collective perception of the moon, its essential beauty and sublime mysteries.

Despite Hollywood and NASA, each of us has some personal concept about the moon. After all, we drop our heads back on any given night and there it is, shaped like a ubiquitous eye or the grin of a Cheshire cat or like a piece of fruit with the top lopped off. It speaks to us. We speak to it. Romance, madness, were-wolves, witches, pagans, Druids, ocean tides and blood tides, or a sharp rise in murder and mayhem: it's all fair game where the moon is concerned. Every notion that we hold about the moon is true *for us,* and that subjective texture is certainly in keeping with the nature of the moon in astrology.

If the sun is where you shine in your corner of the universe, then the moon is your personal oracle. If the sun represents your life force, then the moon represents the internal landscape that supports and maintains the life force. In astrology, lunar energy is embodied in that mythological moment when Luke Skywalker recognizes that Darth Vader is his father or when in *ET* the alien is getting drunk and the boy is trying to dissect a frog at school and their psyches mesh. Lunar energy is operating when reality splits off for the character Gywneth Paltrow plays in *Sliding Doors* or during the love scene in *Titanic*.

Lunar energy is the MO in *Thelma and Louise, Jacob's Ladder,* and *What Dreams May Come*. It's the psychic visions the young boy has in *The Shining* or the visions another young boy has in *The Sixth Sense*.

It's the mother's anguish in *The Deep End of the Ocean,* and it used to be Oprah being Oprah weekday afternoons. Without lunar energy, we would be empty shells, automatons, the burn-the-books society in *Fahrenheit 451.* We would be Keanu Reeves still stuck in the matrix, powerless puppets who accept everything at face value.

Lunar Facts and Oddities

Most of us learn facts about the moon in grade-school science class. Today's kids have a distinct advantage over their parents, of course, because we've already been to the moon, and information is so readily accessible through the Internet.

The moon is our only satellite, and its average distance from Earth is 238,857 miles. Its revolution around the Earth takes 27 days, seven hours, and 43 minutes. Even though it's only a quarter the size of Earth, its gravitational pull is the main cause of our ocean tides. In fact the moon actually has more than twice the effect on tides as the sun.

Since our bodies are primarily water, the moon's gravitational pull on the tides also affects our bodily fluids, metabolic rates, and, of course, our emotions. The link, for instance, between the full moon and violent aggression has been noted for years by police officers, hospital workers, and employees at mental institutions.

In the 1970s a Miami psychiatrist, Arnold Lieber, decided to conduct a scientific study to find out if these observations were true. As a med student at

Jackson Memorial Hospital in Miami, he'd noticed recurring periods when patients on the psyche ward were more disturbed than usual. These periods would last for several days, then the patients would resume their normal behavior. He became curious about the phenomenon and finally conducted a scientific study. His findings, later backed by four other independent studies, confirmed that during the full moon and, to a lesser extent, during the new moon there are increases in all violent crimes—homicide, rape, assault. There's also an increase in lesser crimes—burglary, auto theft, larceny, and drunken and disorderly behavior.

Is it any coincidence, then, that the word *lunatic* is derived from the word *lunar*?

Hospital workers and maternity ward nurses have long noticed that more babies are born at the full and new moons than at any other time of the month. These may be due to the fact that the gravitational pull is strongest when the moon, sun, and Earth are aligned, as they are during the new and full moon. These observations have been backed by scientific studies. Interestingly enough, the lunar calendar is still the basis for calculating a pregnancy. The nine months are synodic months (the length of time it takes the moon to orbit Earth).

Since the moon has no atmosphere, it has nothing to protect it from meteor strikes, which is why its surface is pocked with impact craters. Since it has no tectonic or volcanic activity, its surface is immune to the erosive effects of atmospheric weathering, tectonic shifts, and volcanic upheavals that reshape the surface of our planet. In comparison Earth is a work in progress. On the moon even the footprints left by the

Apollo astronauts will remain intact for millions of years unless a meteor strike obliterates them.

The moon's gravity is about a sixth of ours; that's why the Apollo astronauts looked like they were jumping rope up there. Despite appearances to the contrary, the moon has no light of its own. That gorgeous full moon you see each month is the reflected light of our sun.

In ancient cultures the passage of time was marked according to the lunation—or cycle—of the moon. A *month* was the time between one new moon and the next, and in a typical year there were thirteen lunar cycles. This way of marking time still exists among some pagan sects, and may be closer to our natural rhythms than our present solar calendar.

Astrological Lunar Facts

The moon in your horoscope is every bit as important as your sun sign. In fact, Eastern astrologers give the moon greater emphasis than the sun sign. The moon rules the sign of Cancer and the fourth house in the horoscope. She represents mom or whoever plays that role for you and also symbolizes other women in your life. The moon is feminine, yin, our intuitive selves.

In the physical body her territory pertains primarily to women—breasts, ovaries, womb. In both genders she rules internal fluids and the stomach, and of course she's our emotional barometer, the gauge of our inner health. Not surprisingly, the moon rules conception.

A Czech physician, in fact, theorized that every

woman had a fertility cycle that depended on the phase of the moon when she was born. Eugene Jones developed a fertilization calendar based on his theory, which allegedly showed a 98 percent success rate. He charged an astronomical fee for his calendar, but people who were desperate for children paid it.

Jones claimed that if a woman used his methods, she could choose the gender of her child. His technique was based on the rules of classical astrology, which he'd studied, and boils down to using the gender of moon signs. If conception took place on a Leo day, the child would be male. On a Taurus day the child would be a girl.

The medical establishment went berserk over his claims. But when a panel of gynecologists challenged him to predict the genders of babies based only on their conception dates, Jones' accuracy was 87 percent.

If you don't know the sign of your natal moon, check any of the astrology sites listed in this book and get a free birth chart. You'll need your exact time of birth, place, and of course the date!

The Transiting Moon

The moon changes signs every two and a half days. As you follow along in the daily prediction section for your sign, you'll be able to keep tabs on where the moon is on any given day. Certain activities are favored on certain lunar days, so let's take a look at how you can maximize the transiting moon's energy in your life.

Aries Moon

Cardinal fire sign

This is the day to be a fearless entrepreneur, to move forward on projects that have been sitting on the back burner for weeks or months. It's a great time to initiate new projects too, especially those that have been rattling around in the back of your head for some time.

You may feel restless and impatient with others, so the best way to deal with it is to pour that energy into something about which you feel passionate. Others see you as a leader, as the person with answers. You attract individuals who are eager to be on your team. You feel more self-sufficient, capable of doing whatever needs to be done.

Follow your impulses regardless of how odd they may seem. Sometimes our impulses are the universe's way of leading us toward a new opportunity, a new relationship, a new creative project. Since Mars rules Aries, physical activity is heightened. Take a yoga class. Join the gym. Go walking. Weather permitting, it's a great day for a hike, a bike ride, a long swim.

It's a good day to *believe* that whatever you desire can manifest itself. Your intentions and focus are key.

Taurus Moon

Fixed earth sign

The moon loves Taurus as much as it loves Cancer, the sign that it rules. In Taurus lunar energies work effortlessly, smoothly, and that makes your intuition easier to develop and use.

On a Taurus moon day think about that children's story *Ferdinand the Bull*. The author probably wasn't thinking about Taurus when he created the character, but Ferdinand is the perfect archetype for Taurus. Ferdinand enjoyed peaceful surroundings, and today so do you. In fact, peacefulness and harmony are vital to your emotional well-being. You need these qualities the way a Gemini moon needs books or education or communication with other people.

It will take a lot to anger you today, but repeated provocation can trigger your "bull's rush" fury, the human equivalent of Ferdinand's reaction to the bee sting. Some of the things that can set you off are: incessant nagging by someone who wants you to do something you don't want to do; insistence that you act in a particular way; unreasonable demands or actions by anyone.

A Taurus moon day enables you to stick with something right to the end. You won't be a quitter. You will also be slow to change your mind and opinion and won't be rushed or cajoled into doing something that doesn't interest you.

If you enjoy gardening or have a particular artistic passion, then today is the day to indulge!

Gemini Moon

Mutable air sign

Today your nemesis is boredom. Its possibility unnerves you. If you were put in a bare room without windows, books, TV, radio, computer, paper, pen, phone, fax, or anything else, you would freak within the hour. This may be true of the other air-sign moons as well, but for the Gemini moon it's a sure thing. Your emotional well-being needs mental stimulation and the means to communicate with others.

It's a good day to start blogging, if you haven't already, to dust off that old manuscript you were working on way back when, or to get together with friends and shoot the breeze. You may feel compelled to sign up for a workshop or even an online course in something that interests you. Or you may decide to go to college or graduate school. It's a great day for research, for delving into a topic or concern and finding out everything you can about it.

Communication, whatever form it takes, is paramount.

Cancer Moon

Cardinal water sign

Today your memories work overtime. You're able to conjure sights, smells, tastes, sounds, and textures from your past in vivid detail. The event you're recalling may have happened thirty years ago, but in your memory it's just as fresh and detailed as the day it occurred.

The moon rules Cancer, so it's at home in this sign. This is where its energies express themselves most smoothly. Today your emotions are racing through you, and it may be easy to have your feelings hurt. Your acute sensitivity makes you feel vulnerable, and it isn't easy for you to step back and view a situation or relationship dispassionately.

Family, home, and roots are especially important to you today. Schedule time to be with the people you love. Whether it's a traditional family or friends whom you love like family, you draw comfort and sustenance from these individuals. It's a good time to work on creative projects; your inspiration comes from deep places within you. During the Cancer moon you may have a real soft spot for animals—strays that drop by your place for a bowl of food, the neighbor's cat that sneaks into your house. A visit to your local pound may be in order!

Leo Moon

Fixed fire sign

It's a perfect day to showcase your talents. In fact, when you enter a room, people notice you. If for some reason they don't, then you make sure that they do. This isn't just an ego thing, either. Applause and being noticed are vital to your well-being today even if your only audience is your family. *You need to be recognized as someone special.*

Your flair for drama today is remarkable. It runs through everything you do—from the way you dress, speak, and act to the activities in which you engage. You may decide to take in a play or try out for a part. Creatively, you're at the top of your game, and anything you undertake will bear this dramatic stamp.

It's a good day to spend time with your kids doing something everyone enjoys, to volunteer at an animal shelter, get out and be seen, socialize, make new contacts. Network. Be as flamboyant as you can imagine.

Virgo Moon

Mutable earth sign

Today you're on a quest for perfection and the words *Be the best that you can* take on a whole new dimension of meaning. You thrive on order and manage to use today's lunar energy to tackle emotional chaos in your life and impose order on it.

Virgo tends to be a health-oriented sign, so today favors starting a new diet, nutritional program, exercise regimen. Even if you're already involved in these areas, consider fine-tuning the details. You also may want to consider blogging or writing about what you're learning about health, nutrition, exercise.

Today also favors performing a service for someone else—not for pay, not with any thought of compensation, but as a good deed. This could mean anything from volunteering at your favorite charity to putting in some time at an animal rescue sanctuary. Pay attention to your spiritual beliefs today. Are you in tune with a greater good? Are your thoughts the most positive they can be?

Libra Moon

Cardinal air sign

Among astrologers certain moon signs stir the soul for the sheer beauty of what they represent. The Taurus moon is one of these. The Libra moon is another.

Today, at the heart of it, you're a lover, a true romantic. Moonlit beaches, bouquets of roses, books of poetry, going to the opera, a summer rain: this is the language your soul speaks during the Libra moon. So first of all surround yourself with beauty today—music, scenery, people. Just the sight of all this beauty will deepen your appreciation for life.

It's a good day for group work—in your community or with your students, peers, fellow workers. Or it's a great time to socialize and network. Today your interests tend toward people and relationships, your artistic interests, and attaining peace and harmony. You can see both sides of an issue with greater clarity and try to avoid conflict.

The Libra moon can enhance your intuition, so try to follow your hunches today and see where they lead you. If you don't meditate yet, today is a terrific time to start. It doesn't have to be lengthy. In fact, five minutes in a quiet place with your mind still is all you need. You'll come out of it refreshed. Keep track of any impressions that come your way during those five minutes.

If you're in a committed relationship, then be sure to spend time with your partner. Have a romantic dinner at home or at your favorite restaurant. Talk and get in touch with each other.

Scorpio Moon

Fixed water sign

Emotionally, it's a powerful day. You feel everything so intensely that it's as if some new, inner part of you has awakened from a deep sleep. You may feel as if you've been seized by a force beyond your control. Despite how it feels, this sense of outside forces is just an illusion. Your emotions are your most powerful allies today. They provide you with a direct, immediate connection to the deepest parts of your intuitive self and are capable of instantly transforming your reality.

This transformation happens when you bring your considerable will, intent, and desire to bear against whatever it is that you want to change. When the energy of this moon is focused and backed with passion, this change occurs at the quantum level and can result in the remission of illness or disease, sudden rise in wealth and fame, an explosion of psychic ability . . . well, you get the general idea.

Scorpio is also about power — the power we wield over others and the power others wield over us. All too often this lunar energy is misused or abused when it concerns power issues; then its tremendous capacity for positive transformation becomes negative. The difference seems to be self-awareness.

It's a great day to work with healing energies, intuitive and psychic development, and research and investigation.

Sagittarius Moon

Mutable fire sign

Oh, baby, let the good times roll! For the Sagittarian moon, those good times mean music, deep talk, exotic travel, esoteric ideas. Today you're an explorer. Those explorations may take you to the farther ends of the Earth or deep within the mysteries of the universe. In one way or another this moon enables you to search for the higher truth, the larger picture, a more expansive perspective.

You may be more blunt than usual when dealing with people today, particularly when the other guy just doesn't get what seems so obvious to you. Patience and nuance aren't your strong points during this period. The exception to this occurs when you're pursuing something about which you feel passionate, then you have the patience of Mother Teresa and are as detail oriented as a Virgo.

You're called to action today. You would rather do than think about doing. As a mutable sign, you're emotionally adaptable. You have opinions about virtually everything and aren't the least bit hesitant in expressing these opinions. This becomes a problem if you're dogmatic or bombastic about what you believe and try to convert others to your way of thinking. So today strive to nurture patience and optimism.

Capricorn Moon

Cardinal earth sign

The moon isn't particularly comfortable in this sign. It chafes at all the rules and restrictions that Capricorn seeks to impose and dislikes all that earthy grounding. However, this moon certainly favors strategy—laying out goals and figuring ways to achieve them. Your physical energy is excellent today and enables you to work long hours to meet a deadline, regardless of whether that deadline is self-imposed (which it often is) or imposed by a boss.

You feel quite independent today and may find yourself outdoors, hiking alone through the wilderness or at the gym, putting in extra time on the treadmill. Under this lunar influence, you push yourself, move the bar higher, and feel a certain determination to carve your niche in the larger world.

Today it's easier to categorize your emotions, to look at things dispassionately. So tackle stuff that pushes your buttons, issues that you've pushed aside but which beg for a resolution.

Aquarius Moon

Fixed air sign

Today you march to a different drummer. You may hear a different kind of music in your very cells and feel compelled to decipher the message and act on it. This is the sign, after all, that ushers in new paradigms by refusing to go along with the status quo.

The visionary component to this moon sign gives you an edge today on new trends. You can spot the next wave long before anyone else does. The trick is acting on it and putting it to work for you in your personal and professional life. Your rational mind may try to intervene, to argue and put up blocks, to keep you within the confining box of consensus reality. Or someone close to you—a parent, close friend, significant other—inadvertently plays that role, and you suddenly find yourself on the defensive.

So today be fearless. Go forward secure in the knowledge that your vision is correct!

Pisces Moon

Mutable water sign

Today you're the archetypal dreamer, your feet never really firmly rooted on the earth. You're deeply compassionate today too, a true bleeding heart. You probably won't be able to pass a homeless person on the street without giving him money, and you definitely won't resist the soulful gaze of a stray pup or kitten. Injustices of any sort may fill you with a deep sadness. Your challenge during this moon is to detach emotionally from situations and people who cause you this kind of anguish.

Part of the problem is that today you're a psychic sponge who soaks up the emotions and moods of the people around you. This alone makes it vital that you associate with upbeat, positive people and situations that boost your energy rather than sap it.

The Pisces moon favors imagination, intuition, any artistic endeavor. On a strictly mundane level it's a fine day to shop for new clothes, get a new hairdo, redesign yourself in some way. Also, your dreams should be especially vivid and could contain important insights and information.

CHAPTER 9

Money, Luck, and Synchronicity in 2013

Money and luck don't necessarily go hand in hand. Vast fortunes are often made because the individual had vision and was able to make that vision a concrete reality. Sometimes people are simply in the right place at the right time and play their cards exactly right. Usually synchronicity plays a major role. Let's take a closer look.

The word, coined by Swiss psychiatrist Carl Jung, means the coming together of inner and outer events in a way that is meaningful to the observer and can't be explained by cause and effect. Or: meaningful co-incidence. We've all experienced these events. You're thinking of a friend you haven't seen for years, and suddenly you get an invite from that person on Face-book. Or you're delayed on your way to work one morning, and when you finally arrive at your turnoff discover there was an accident at just about the time you would have driven through if you'd been on time.

Once you're aware that these incidents hold a deeper meaning, they tend to happen more frequently. As you begin to work with these synchronicities, deciphering their messages, you suddenly realize you're in the flow, in the right place at the right time.

The planet that can help us get into the flow—Jupiter—is also the planet that represents luck and expansion, success, prosperity, growth, creativity, spiritual interests, higher education, and the law. It also governs publishing, overseas travel, and foreign countries and our dealings with them. This year it will be in two signs. Between January 1 and June 25, it will be transiting air sign Gemini. Between June 25, 2013, and July 16, 2014, it will be transiting Cancer. Let's take a look at how these transits might attract more synchronicity, luck, and prosperity into your life this year.

Aries

If you aren't aware of synchronicity, then your best time this year for delving into this fascinating phenomenon is between January 1 and June 25, while Jupiter in Gemini moves through your solar third house of communication. You may want to keep a journal about your experiences as the synchros occur and to note what types of synchronicities they are. Do they occur in clusters, with the same name, word, or phrase happening repeatedly during a relatively short period of time? Do your experiences act as guidance, confirmation, warnings?

It's relatively easy for you to get into the flow, Aries. Just follow your impulses. They often lead you to exactly where you need to be. If you have a hunch that you should follow a particular course, by all means follow the hunch. If a dream provides what seems to be information about an issue that concerns you, be sure to consider this information before making a decision. Financially, if you are careful about impulse spending, you should do well during Jupiter's transit of Gemini. Be sure to pay attention to Mercury retrograde periods, however, and avoid buying large-ticket items during those times.

Between June 25, 2013, and July 16, 2014, when Jupiter is in Cancer, you can easily apply what you've learned during the previous six months. Your home life/domestic environment may be expanding in some way, so be sure to watch for synchros in that area. Your intuition will increase, and your hunches should proliferate during this period.

Taurus

Your finances should be expanding during the first six months of the year. In fact, if money is your focus, then it's likely your synchronicities will occur within the financial area. You may discover, for instance, that you have a hunch to buy a particular stock, and when you follow the hunch the stock rises within a day. Later when someone asks why you bought that particular stock, you won't really know why, except that you *had a feeling*.

During Jupiter's transit through Cancer you're going to be in a strong position to talk about your synchronicities, your luck, how your life is expanding. You may want to blog about it, to reach out to other like-minded individuals. Your capacity for communication will expand appreciably during this year-long transit. Your intuition should be exceptionally strong too, particularly as it relates to your neighborhood and community.

Gemini

When Jupiter transits your sign during the first six months of 2013, your life will be expanding in numerous directions. One of those areas will be your finances. Be sure to stay on top of things, Gemini, especially if the money is rolling in faster than you can count it. Check and recheck your bank statements, stocks, investment portfolio, 401K contributions, even pay stubs. Don't be obsessive about it, just take responsibility for where your money goes and how you spend it.

During this transit you won't just *feel* lucky, you'll actually *be* lucky. Your optimism and generally positive outlook on life will attract what you need before you need it. New people and opportunities will enter your life, and you'll have plenty of choices to make. All the stuff that unfolds during the first six months of 2013 prepares you for Jupiter's transit of Cancer and your financial area between June 25, 2013, and July 16, 2014. Initially this transit may bring about some hefty expenditures, but sometimes you have to spend money to make money! By mid-July 2014 your financial affairs will be looking quite grand.

Cancer

During the first half of the year Jupiter transits your solar twelfth house. This period brings heightened insights concerning your own psyche and unconscious. You may try therapy, take up meditation. Jupiter's transit through Gemini makes your unconscious more accessible to you in some way, and you discuss the process with others through a blog or Web site, by writing a book, keeping a journal. You may even work this process into your professional life in some way. One purpose for this transit is to clear out the old to make way for the new when Jupiter enters your sign. You may be discarding beliefs that no longer serve your best interests, breaking longstanding habits. Relationships may end, but new ones begin.

By the time Jupiter enters Cancer on June 25, you're ready for the adventure, whatever it may be. Your financial picture should expand considerably—a plump raise, a new business venture, royalties. Your intuition is greatly enhanced during this transit, and you're able to create a rich psychic environment for synchronicity. Be sure to decipher the messages of these synchros; they hold valuable information for you.

Leo

The first Jupiter transit this year expands your circle of friends, acquaintances, and connections. You're able to network effectively and find the support you need for new projects and ventures. You may experience synchronicities that involve other people. You might, for instance, dream of someone you know you've never met—only to meet that same person the next day or a week later. Any seeds you sow during this transit will be beneficial down the line, Leo. Since the transit occurs in Gemini, consider putting up a Web site or starting a blog on a topic about which you're passionate.

During the second transit, which lasts about a year, you're journeying through your own unconscious, which is more readily accessible to you. It's similar to what Cancer experiences when Jupiter transits its twelfth house, but with an important difference. Cancer enjoys solitude; you generally don't. So for you this transit can best be used by joining a meditation class or taking up yoga or tai chi. In other words, get involved with classes, where you have people around you. Your synchros during this period may involve guidance on issues you must settle before Jupiter enters your sign in mid-2014.

Virgo

The first part of the year focuses on an expansion in your career, Virgo. You might get promoted, land a nice raise, change jobs or careers to something that suits you better. Synchronicities you experience may revolve around career issues and concerns. Be sure to decode the messages that come with these synchros; they could prove helpful as guidance and confirmation. Your precision and attention to detail during this time should aid you if you assume a lot of responsibility, as you're apt to do.

During the second Jupiter transit, which lasts about a year, you'll really be in your element. Friends, acquaintances, and social groups will be lucky for you, and your social circle should expand tremendously. The connections you make will prove to be beneficial and will expand your worldview in some way. Synchronicities, once you're aware of them, should come fast and furiously, and you won't have any trouble deciphering them. Your particular mindset lends itself to solving puzzles and mysteries.

Libra

During the first six months of the year, while Jupiter transits fellow air sign Gemini, your opportunities for expansion should be remarkable. The ninth house governs your worldview, higher education, publishing, and foreign travel, so expansions are likely to take place in those areas. Your communication opportunities should expand as well. You might sell a book or novel you've written, might go to college or graduate school, may sign up for a seminar or workshop on a topic about which you're passionate. If you travel a great deal during this period, don't be surprised if you begin to experience a flurry of synchronicities.

While Jupiter transits Cancer between June 25, 2013, and July 16, 2014, it will be moving through your career area. This period should be exciting, with your professional opportunities multiplying almost more quickly than you can keep up with. You'll be lucky professionally—you're the right person at the right time and place, that sort of lucky. You may change jobs or careers, and if you do, it's for a better position and more pay. You could also be promoted or may decide to launch your own business.

Scorpio

During Jupiter's transit through Gemini and your solar eighth house (until June 25, 2013) your partner's income will expand, and you may be delving more deeply into metaphysics. Your intuitive abilities should deepen considerably under this transit—and you're already one of the most psychic signs in the zodiac! You may be researching and investigating life after death, communication with spirits, haunted houses, things that go bump in the night. You'll be fortunate with mundane things as well—mortgages, loans, taxes, insurance, all of which falls under the eighth house.

Jupiter's transit through fellow water sign Cancer—June 25, 2013, to July 16, 2014—will be very much to your liking, Scorpio. This one should expand your opportunities for foreign travel and broadening your worldview and spiritual beliefs. You may sample different religions or spiritual beliefs, launch a spiritual quest, even travel to far-flung locales in search of spiritual truths. It all depends, Scorpio, on what you're seeking and how sincere you are in your desires.

Sagittarius

Since Jupiter rules your sign, its movements impact you quite personally and powerfully. During the first six months, when Jupiter transits your opposite, Gemini, your partnership opportunities increase. You may find exactly the right business or romantic partner or both. If you're involved in a relationship, then you may decide to deepen your commitment—move in together, get engaged, or marry. Synchronicities you experience are likely to be related to partnerships and issues concerning commitment and communication.

Between June 25, 2013, and July 16, 2014, Jupiter transits Cancer and your solar eighth house. The eighth house dynamics are always intriguing. On one side you have mundane issues—taxes, insurance, bank loans, and mortgages—and on the other side you have esoteric stuff — hauntings, life after death, communication with the dead. These issues will be focal points for expansion. Synchronicities are likely to abound in these areas. It should be easier for you to obtain a mortgage and bank loan, and you will find yourself drawn to explore things that go bump in the night. You may even travel abroad to investigate crop circles or UFO reports. It all depends on how far outside the box your interests extend.

Capricorn

During the first six months of the year, when Jupiter is transiting Gemini and your solar sixth house, your responsibilities at work increase. You may be putting in longer hours, but enjoying your work more. Your communication with coworkers and employees is more frequent and lively, and you find camaraderie with coworkers who think along the same lines that you do.

If you've been unemployed, then this transit should help you land a job that not only pays the bills, but which makes you feel more optimistic generally about your life. Despite what you see around you in terms of financial hardships others may be experiencing, your world feels more secure.

Once Jupiter enters Cancer, your opposite sign (June 25, 2013, to July 16, 2014), your partnership opportunities increase. If you're involved in a relationship already, then you and your partner may move in together, get engaged, or marry. Professional partnerships are also impacted by this transit. Let's say you've started your own business but may be lacking in the financial department until the business gets off the ground. Jupiter in Cancer helps you find the right partner, at the right time.

Synchronicities tend to happen more frequently when we're in transitional phases of our lives, so pay attention to them. They can guide you and act as confirmation for your choices.

Aquarius

While Jupiter is in fellow air sign Gemini, you're in a very good place, Aquarius. The first six months of the year should bring expansion in the areas of romance, creativity, and everything you do for pleasure. If you've thought about starting a family, then Jupiter in Gemini and your solar fifth house could help bring that about. If you weren't involved when this transit began last year, then you probably are now and are thoroughly enjoying yourself. Creatively, you're on a definite roll. Your muse is whispering to you 24/7, and you awaken each morning with a song in your heart, eager to embrace the day.

Between June 25, 2013, and July 16, 2014, Jupiter moves through water sign Cancer and your solar sixth house. This transit brings an expansion in your daily work. You may land a promotion, get a raise, hire new employees for your business, spend more time socializing with coworkers. With Jupiter in the nurturing sign of Cancer, you may experience an expansion in your domestic situation too. Perhaps a parent moves in or a child moves back home after college. You may build an addition to your home.

Synchronicities come in all shapes and forms. Don't

dismiss any meaningful coincidence as just random weirdness. Take a deeper look; decipher the message.

Pisces

Jupiter corules your sign, so its transits are always significant for you. During the first six months, while Jupiter transits Gemini and your solar fourth house, your domestic situation expands in some way. Perhaps your significant other moves in with you. Or you and your partner have a child. Or a parent moves in. Or, equally possible, you may move—across town, across the country, or to another country.

Between June 25, 2013, and July 16, 2014, Jupiter transits fellow water sign Cancer, and you're in the driver's seat, Pisces. This transit bolsters your imagination, creative abilities, and capacity for enjoyment. Love and romance are tops on your list, and you have no shortage of opportunities in these areas. Synchronicities are likely to swirl through your life during this transit, and because you're so innately psychic you get the message easily.

CHAPTER 10

The Thirteenth Sign

On January 10, 2011, the *Minneapolis Star Tribune* carried an article about the emergence of a possible thirteenth zodiac sign. The story apparently zipped around cyberspace at the speed of light and was picked up by CNN, ABC, and NBC. Network coverage on this topic struck me as weird: since when do they cover astrology?

It was covered because an astronomer—not an astrologer—made the announcement about the thirteenth sign and presented a new set of dates for all the signs, shifting the zodiac. Paul Kunkle, who teaches astronomy at a junior college in Minneapolis, pointed out that the zodiac periods were set up by the Babylonians millennia ago. Since then the moon's gravitational pull has made the Earth "wobble" on its axis, which has created a one-month difference in the stars' alignment over time. "When astrologers say the sun is in Pisces, it's really not in Pisces," said Kunkle. "Most horoscope readers who consider themselves Pisces are actually Aquarians."

Here's how the dates line up under Kunkle's theory:

Aries: April 18–May 13
Taurus: May 13–June 21
Gemini: June 21–July 20
Cancer: July 20–August 10
Leo: August 10–September 16
Virgo: September 16–October 30
Libra: October 30–November 23
Scorpio: November 23–November 29
Ophiuchus: November 29–December 17
Sagittarius: December 17–January 20
Capricorn: January 20–February 16
Aquarius: February 16–March 11
Pisces: March 11–April 18

Notice the new sign for November 29 to December 17? That's Ophiuchus (OFF-ee-YOO-kuss), the Serpent Bearer, which in Kunkle's view now belongs in the mainstream zodiac.

However, Kunkle's dates are irrelevant for Western astrology; he's actually referring to sidereal astrology, which is oriented to the constellations. Tropical astrology, the most common form in the Western world, is based on the seasons. It's geocentric—related to life on Earth. In tropical astrology, if you were born between February 19 and March 20, you're still a Pisces!

The irony is that the ancient Babylonians knew about Ophiuchus, but because they didn't want a zodiac with thirteen signs they tossed it out. They supposedly thought that thirteen wasn't as tidy as twelve. It was one of the forty-eight constellations listed by the second-century astronomer Ptolemy and is one of the eighty-eight modern constellations. As you can see, though Ophiuchus may be new to us, it has been around for centuries.

But what should we make of its recent reappearance in the astrological conversation? Perhaps, in a larger context, its rediscovery signals the emergence of a new planetary archetype, and its importance can be found in what it might be telling us about humanity and ourselves at this juncture in time. That's where synchronicity enters the picture.

Planets are archetypes—Mars, for instance, is the mythological god of war; Venus is the mythological goddess of love. A planet's discovery often "coincides" with a shift in mass consciousness that comes about as certain world events and situations unfold. For example, in 1930 a new planet was discovered as a result of aberrations in the orbit of Uranus. The planet was named Pluto, after the god of the underworld. In mythology Pluto is associated with Hades— hell—and with immense power and destruction. In Latin literature Pluto also rules the dead. In astrology this planet came to be associated with profound and irrevocable change, transformation, strange taboos, dictators, decadence, disasters, atomic power, gangsters (Mafia), sexuality, the sexual act, sexual power, death, dying, rebirth, explosions, power struggles . . . you get the idea.

The world events surrounding its discovery included two world wars, the emergence of atomic weapons, the rise of Nazis and Hitler, concentration camps, and the annihilation of six million Jews and minority groups. It also saw the birth of psychoanalysis, notably the work of Sigmund Freud, which focuses on sexuality, and Carl Jung, whose work deals with mythology, dreams, archetypes, and synchronicity. So what kind of archetype might be emerging with the *rediscovery* of Ophiuchus?

Well, it's the only astrological sign based on a real person: Asclepius. By the ancient Greeks in 27 B.C. he was regarded as a healer, and in the Roman pantheon he is a son of Apollo. He supposedly learned the secrets of preventing death when he observed one serpent bringing healing herbs to another. He raised the dead using this herb. In order to prevent the entire human race from becoming immortal under his care, Zeus supposedly killed him with a bolt of lightning, then later suffered a pang of conscience and placed his image in the heavens to honor his good works.

Ophiuchus is usually depicted as grasping a snake—thus his name as the Serpent Bearer—and has one foot resting firmly against Scorpius (the scorpion). In honor of Asclepius, snakes were often used in healing rituals, and nonvenomous snakes were allowed to crawl on the floor in dormitories where the sick and injured slept. Cults grew up around Asclepius in Greece and Rome, and pilgrims supposedly flocked to his healing temples from 300 B.C. onward. Ritual purification would be followed by offerings or sacrifices to the gods and by spending the night in the holiest part of the sanctuary so that dreams would occur. Any dreams or visions were reported to a priest, who would prescribe the appropriate therapy by interpreting what the dreams meant.

Just from the mythology we can glimpse some of the components of the archetype: healer, alternative medicine, the power of groups (pilgrims flocking to the temples), magic (raising the dead), dream interpretation, cult mentality, violence and violent deaths, sudden unexpected events (thunderbolts), resisting and questioning authority, pushing against the status quo, a greater independence from authoritarian rule (sounds like what has been going on in Egypt and the Middle East and North Africa in general), and greater dependence on the self and the local community.

Other components of this archetype include what author and physician Dean Radin calls "the global mind, the collective consciousness of everyone on the planet." This phrase grew out of Radin's involvement in the Global Consciousness Project. In 1998 Princeton's Dr. Roger Nelson, in conjunction with the Institute of Noetic Sciences, began an Internet-based experiment aimed at monitoring this global mind. Through dozens of random number generators situated worldwide, the idea is that "as mind moves, so does matter" (Dean Radin). The findings so far are intriguing.

Networks of random number generators are present at sixty-five sites worldwide. Once a minute the generated numbers are downloaded and analyzed for consistency. The process is explained in detail on the project's Web site: www.gcpdot.com. The purpose of the project, according to the Web site, is "to examine subtle correlations that may reflect the presence and activity of consciousness in the world. We predict structure in what should be random data, associated with major world events."

So during events that are of global interest, the focused attention and emotional outpouring worldwide brings about a notable difference in the results. The Web site maintains a GCP dot that registers these fluctuations in the global mind in real time, covered 24/7 by the media. Hours before the first plane hit the World Trade Center, these random number generators went a bit nuts, and the button turned red. If you read what it says about colors on the Global Consciousness Project Web site, you'll see that red indicates a variance in the statistical analysis of these generators—an event that mass consciousness registers, sometimes before the event occurs it seems. The same thing happened during the original O.J. Simpson trial and shortly before the Tucson shootings involving Representative Gabrielle Giffords earlier this year. In other words, these generators registered the fluctuations in consciousness.

Magnetic fluctuation impacts human beings, and it may be creating a sensitivity in certain types of individuals, which is part of this emerging paradigm. Planetary empaths are individuals who seem to be so intimately connected to fluctuations in the earth that they experience physical symptoms for days and sometimes weeks before a natural disaster occurs. Their "symptoms" are astonishingly similar and often coincide with the change in colors in the GCP dot. One woman in California, for instance, knows that when her left ear starts ringing and throbbing painfully, an earthquake is imminent. Another woman is seized by vertigo before a quake.

There's no question a paradigm shift of some sort is underway. This shift in mass consciousness may be what the rediscovery of Ophiuchus presages.

That said, there are troubling facts emerging that suggest this paradigm shift may occur *as a result of* global warming, an increase in natural disasters, a widening disparity between rich and poor, and increased political and religious strife worldwide. We've covered some of the facts in other posts—about the massive deaths of birds and other wildlife, for instance. Here are some additional facts:

- In 2010 natural disasters killed more than a quarter of a million people and displaced millions. According to Swiss Re, the largest reinsurer in the world, the financial losses from these natural disasters exceeded two hundred and twenty-two billion dollars.
- Greenland's ice sheet melted at a record rate in 2010.
- 2005 and 2010 are tied for the warmest years on record.
- The last pole shift occurred nearly 800,000 years ago. Some scientists believe we're long overdue. Others believe a pole shift is already underway.

So this rediscovery of Ophiuchus may be a warning, or it may be prompting us to really examine our collective beliefs and desires. What do we *want* not only for ourselves and our loved ones, but for the planet?

CHAPTER 11

The Astro Neighborhood

If you Google *astrology,* more than 40 million links show up. Perhaps in uncertain times people are looking for information and insights through nontraditional sources. Or maybe astrology has gone mainstream!

You can find sites for virtually any aspect of this fascinating field, but some sites are far superior and more user friendly than others. These sites offer free natal charts, daily transits, monthly horoscopes, and political and world predictions. It's all at your fingertips. Here are the sites we consider to be the best:

www.astrologyzone.com: Susan Miller's site is a favorite for neophytes and pros alike. Every month she writes about 3,000 words per sign, with detailed predictions for the month. She cites the best days for romance, finances, and career matters. She discusses new and full moons, eclipses and their impact on your sun sign, and provides information on various aspects that are coming up in a given month. You can also obtain a free natal chart. Her site is chocked with information and is user friendly, and her predictions are eerily accurate.

www.astro.com: This site is also jammed with information. Here you can get a free natal chart, see immediately where the planets are today, use the ephemeris, and find out the geographical coordinates for a particular city. There are other interesting tidbits as well—celebrities born on a given day and fascinating and informative articles by some of the world's best astrologers. This site is perfect for the beginner, the intermediary, and the advanced astrologer.

www.moonvalleyastrologer.com: Celeste Teal is *the* expert on eclipses, a specialized area of astrology that few have researched the way she has. Her two books on eclipses are seminal works. She also provides informative articles on various aspects of astrology. If you're new to astrology, there's plenty on this site to whet your appetite. Regardless of your expertise in astrology, Celeste's site offers information for everyone.

www.astrocollege.com: Lois Rodden's site is extraordinary. This woman spent most of her life collecting birth data and then created a piece of software that is invaluable in research. For example, you can compare charts of individuals in virtually any field and discover what astrological components they have in common. Let's say you're looking for artists who all had Leo suns, Capricorn moons, and Scorpio rising. You enter those criteria, and the software delivers names. The software also provides *signatures*—a certain combination of aspects and other factors that point to particular characteristics in an individual. In addition, the site rates and sells astrology software. Lois has passed on, but her work survives.

http://astrofuturetrends.com: Author and astrologer Anthony Louis does just what the site says. He predicts future trends, covers political stuff, and provides an overall view of astrology.

www.starlightnews.com: Click on Nancy's blog. Here you'll find the latest predictions and insights about world affairs. Nancy's predictions about politics have been right on. Before the 2004 election she made some predictions about tight senatorial races that were totally accurate. She also called the presidential race in 2008. We've been following her closely ever since. She receives hundreds of comments for her posts, and some of them are as informative as her posts.

www.ofscarabs.blogspot.com: About synchronicities—what they are, how they show up in our lives, what they might mean, and hundreds of stories. There are occasional posts on astrological factors, like Mercury retrograde!

Software

In the days before computers a natal chart or anything else connected to astrology had to be configured manually, through complicated mathematical formulas that left you gasping. Astrology software has truly transformed the study of astrology and our knowledge about it. Since the late 1980s, when we began using astrology software, the choices have multiplied.

Our first piece of software was a really simple program we found at a computer store for ten bucks. It erected a chart in about sixty seconds. There it was, rising, moon, sun, planets, the houses, everything set up on the computer screen as if by magic. In the late

1990s we bought our first really terrific astrology software from Matrix for about $300. In the years since http://www.astrologysoftware.com has supplied us with endless data and information and revolutionized the study of astrology.

But it's not just enough to have a great piece of software. When your computer crashes, when you receive updates that screw up, when windows updates to a new system, you call the Matrix help line, and their people walk you through it until everything works. And the employees on their help lines aren't outsourced. You won't reach India. You'll talk to someone in Michigan who is not only an astrologer, but a computer geek who knows how to fix your problem. If by some fluke they can't fix your problem, they'll credit you for one of their other terrific programs.

The only complaint we have about Matrix is that to activate the software, you have to call or contact them through the Internet to receive a special code. If your computer crashes, if you buy a new PC or laptop . . . well, it's annoying. When you pay this much for software, you shouldn't have to obtain a special access code.

Another great piece of software is **SolarFire**. Astrologers are as dedicated to this program as they are to Matrix's software. Check out http://www.alabe.com for current prices. While the two programs offer similar features and capabilities, preferences seem to be individual. Both Matrix's Winstar and astrolabe's SolarFire offer many of the same features—natal charts, transits, progressed charts, solar charts, and interpretations. They both feature material about fixed stars, aspects, lunations, eclipses, and all the other important components you could possibly want or need. The main difference lies in the appearance of the charts and how the information is presented.

Kepler's astrology program — http://www.astrosoft ware.com — is beautiful in its rendition of charts, interpretations, and just about anything any astrologer could use or need. We like it for its ease, its beauty. But it lacks the complexity of both Winstar and SolarFire. The program simply doesn't do as much.

If your exploration of astrology takes you deeper, there are other software programs that help get you there. Bernadette Brady is the undisputed mistress of fixed stars. Her software program, *Starlight,* is remarkable not only for its accuracy but for its presentation. You will never think of fixed stars in the same way once you play with this program. What won't make sense in a natal chart interpretation suddenly snaps into clarity when you use her software. Be sure to download a print to file version for the software — through a PDF file — so that you can maximize usage. Their website: http://www.zyntara.com.

Lois Rodden's AstroDatabank is the software that Lois Rodden developed. It contains over 30,000 birth records, "carefully documented and coded for accuracy with the popular Rodden Rating system. Astro-Databank includes intriguing biographies, revealing personality traits, important life events, and significant relationships." For the curious, the researcher, the neophyte, and pro alike.

Both Winstar and SolarFire produce computerized report software. These reports are handy for when a friend of a friend is in a fix, and you don't have the time to interpret transits and progressions for the person's birth chart. Winstar also produces software on other divination systems.

Day Watch, another Winstar program, is forecasting software that is invaluable for astrologers. From their site: "Certainly it creates personalized astrological calendars, a great tool for professional astrologers and those who have an understanding of astrological terms, symbols, and technique. But Day Watch also contains a full range of onscreen and printable interpretations of events that even someone with absolutely no astrological training can read, understand, and immediately put to use in their daily lives."

Io/Edition Graphic Astrology is the only astrology software for Macs. It's basic, but better than not having any software at all.

At the beginning of every month we bring up our personalized calendars, which tell us what is happening daily in our natal charts and also lists which planets are changing signs in that month, on what date, and which planets are turning retrograde or direct. Each month includes an ephemeris and lunar charts for the new and full moon. The program also offers various types of reports.

Getting a Reading

So now you're ready for an astrological reading. But where do you start? Which astrologer should you use?

The best way to find an astrologer is through someone who has gotten a reading and recommends the individual. If you don't know anyone who has had an astrological reading, then the next best course is to head over to the nearest bookstore and look through the astrology books. Browse through titles that interest you. Note the author's style. If the author uses a lot of astro jargon or seems to write in a depressing or heavy-handed way, move on. Once you find an author whose book you like, check to see if he or she has a Web site. Most astrologers these days have Web sites that spell out their fees, what types of readings are offered, and a contact address.

Rates for a reading vary from one astrologer to another and usually depend on what you want. Would you like just an interpretation of your natal chart? Would you like a forecast for the next six months or a year? Do you want a compatibility chart for you and your partner? Some astrologers prefer to do phone readings, and record the reading. Others prefer to work through e-mail. If the astrologer you've chosen lives close to you, all the better. Have the reading done in person.

What to Expect During a Reading

Every astrological reading begins with your natal chart, so an accurate birth time is essential. It should come from your birth certificate or a parent's memory. An approximate time means the entire reading won't be as accurate. Over the years we've done way too many readings that turned out to be based on inaccurate birth times and then had to construct an accurate chart. If you don't know your time of birth, it's possible to rectify your chart based on major events in your life—the date of your marriage or divorce, a major move, the death of a parent. But this process is time consuming and rarely as accurate as an exact birth time.

A reading with an astrologer differs from a daily horoscope you find in a newspaper or even on a Web site. It's tailored to your specific chart rather than just to your sun sign. If you're getting a reading only on your birth chart, then the astrologer interprets the entire chart, not just pieces of it. The astrologer looks at the signs and house placements of the various planets and the angles the planets make to each other.

If you want predictions for the next six or twelve months, the astrologer uses various techniques that are all based on your natal chart. Transits—the daily motion of the planets—have the most immediate impact on our lives, so the astrologer will first look at how the slower-moving planets (Pluto, Neptune, Uranus) impact your chart. Since they stay in the same sign for the greatest length of time, their influence can be felt for decades. The transits of the other planets are also taken into account, of course. Usually the astrologer will pay close attention to how the transits of your chart's ruler are affecting you. If you have Scorpio rising, then the transits of Pluto and Mars (the coruler) would be important. If you have Gemini rising, then Mercury's transits would be important. The astrologer should also consider how eclipses and the new and full moons might affect you, particularly when there's a lunation in the same sign as your natal sun, moon, or rising.

Another predictive technique the astrologer should use is one called progression. In this technique your natal chart is progressed forward in time to the present. Since the moon is the swiftest-moving planet, moving about one progressed degree a month, the progressed chart provides timing. An astrologer can time events down to a month.

Yet another predictive technique is called the solar return chart, where your sun sign is returned to where it was at your birth. This chart's influence extends from one birthday to the next and when compared with the natal chart provides additional information and insights about what you can expect during the next twelve months.

An astrologer may also take a look at other elements in your chart or, if you have a specific question, can erect an horary chart for that particular question. Horary astrology is a specialized field, and not all astrologers are competent to answer questions using this technique.

CHAPTER 12

By the Numbers

Even though this is an astrology book, we use numbers in some of the daily predictions because we're attempting to remain true to what Sydney Omarr did. The legendary astrologer was also a numerologist and combined the two forms in his work. So let's take a closer look at how the numbers work.

If you're familiar with numerology, you probably know your life path number, which is derived from your birth date. That number represents who you were at birth and the traits that you'll carry throughout your life. There are numerous books and Web sites that provide details on what the numbers mean regarding your life path.

But in the daily predictions, what does it mean when it's a number 9 day, and how did it get to be that number? In the dailies you'll usually find these numbers on the days when the moon is transiting from one sign to another. The system is simple: add the numbers related to the astrological sign (1 for Aries, 2 for Taurus, etc.), the year, the month, and the day.

For example, to find what number June 14, 2011, is

for a Libra, you would start with 7, the number for Libra, add 4 (the number you get when you add 2011 together), plus 6 for June, plus 5 (1+4) for the day. That would be 7+4+6+5 (sign + year + month+ day) = 22=4. So June 14, 2011, is a number 4 day for a Libra. It would be a 5 day for a Scorpio, the sign following Libra. So on that number 4 day, Libra might be advised that her organizational skills are highlighted, that she should stay focused, get organized, be methodical and thorough. She's building a creative future. Tear down the old in order to rebuild. Keep your goals in mind; follow your ideas.

Briefly, here are the meanings of the numbers, which are included in more detail in the dailies themselves.

1) Taking the lead, getting a fresh start, a new beginning
2) Cooperation, partnership, a new relationship, sensitivity
3) Harmony, beauty, pleasures of life, warm, receptive
4) Getting organized, hard work, being methodical, rebuilding, fulfilling your obligations
5) Freedom of thought and action, change, variety, thinking outside the box
6) A service day, being diplomatic, generous, tolerant, sympathetic
7) Mystery, secrets, investigations, research, detecting deception, exploration of the unknown, of the spiritual realms
8) Your power day, financial success, unexpected money, a windfall

9) Finishing a project, looking beyond the immediate, setting your goals, reflection, expansion.

Simple, right?

Once you become accustomed to what the numbers mean for a particular day, you can adjust your attitude and thoughts accordingly. After all, how a day or week, month or year unfolds depends more on your attitude toward yourself and your world than it does on any number or astrology sign. If you practice waking up each morning in a spirit of adventure and gratitude, then pretty soon it becomes second nature, and your life shifts accordingly. Sound like magical thinking? It is. Try it, and watch your life change.

CHAPTER 13

Romance and Timing for Cancer in 2013

For the Single Cancer

Timing. The best part of astrology is about timing. When is it a favorable time to meet someone? When is the best time to get engaged or married? When is the best time to move, sell your home, start a new job? In terms of romance and love, we look to the transits of Venus first.

Venus, as the planet that symbolizes love, romance, the arts, creativity, money, is considered, along with Jupiter, to be one of the beneficial planets. So we look at the signs it transits, which house Venus is transiting, and whether it's making a harmonious or challenging angle to your sun and other planets. We also look at Mars, symbolic of your sexual and physical energy, and Mercury, symbolic of communication, and the signs and houses they are transiting and the angles they're making to other planets. We look for propitious new and full moons, and also take into account what the larger planets are doing.

So let's take a closer look at the dates to watch for in 2013 that favor romance, love, creative endeavors.

June 2–27. Venus is in your sign, Cancer. This period brings renewed and soaring self-confidence, your presence appeals to others, and bosses and co-workers (and just about everyone else) are open to your ideas and creative endeavors. Keep your social calendar wide open during this period, accept social invitations, get out and be seen. You won't meet anyone if you're sitting at home watching TV or surfing the Internet.

Your passions run high during this period. You're attracted to people with whom you share an intuitive connection. Your intuition is especially powerful during this transit, so pay attention to your hunches! Since your muse is at your beck and call 24/7 right now, be sure to indulge your creative interests. By doing what you enjoy during this transit, your chances are increased of meeting someone with whom you share an instant camaraderie.

September 11–October 7. During this period Venus is in that area of your chart that symbolizes romance, love, creativity and children. It's one of the most romantic and creative periods for you all year. With Venus in passionate Scorpio, it's also one of the most emotionally intense periods. If you're uninvolved at the beginning of the transit, you probably won't be when the transit ends. But if you are, it won't make much difference. You're having too much fun and are deeply involved in creative projects.

February 25–March 21. Venus transits Pisces, your solar ninth house. This transit stimulates romance and love while traveling. Or, equally possible, you meet someone at a workshop, seminar, or class who piques your interest. This transit, like the others through fellow water signs, deepens your intuition and imagination.

For the Partnered Cancer

Whether you and your partner are married, living together, or just getting to know each other, the above dates should be beneficial for the relationship. Let's find out how.

June 2–27. With Venus in your sign, your self-confidence is humming along at a perfect pitch, and others find your presence intriguing, attractive. Others like your ideas, everything you have to say. Your partner, in particular, is paying more attention to you; they may bring meaningful gifts or call you unexpectedly. Little gestures mean a lot now. The two of you are intuitively connected during this transit, the kind of thing where one completes what the other is about to say.

The only drawback to this transit is that you may have a tendency to be clingy, demanding all your partner's time and attention. Instead, be loving toward your partner but without possessiveness.

September 11–October 7. This is when you discover your capacity for love, being romanced, joining with your partner in a creative project of some kind. During this period you're in love with the idea of love, with the idea of meaningful conversations about the scope of life, the universe, and your relationship. You enjoy the sensual pleasures of your relationship and are intent on spending quality time with your partner, doing what you both enjoy.

February 25–March 21. You and your partner hit the road—either literally or figuratively. You may actually take off on a trip together, or you might dive into a metaphysical exploration of some kind. If you combine the two, then your journey may be a kind of mutual quest. Allow synchronicity to be your compass.

For All Cancers

Women may be from Venus and men from Mars, but both planets have plenty to tell us about our psychological makeup when it comes to relationships.

Venus represents our capacity for love, how we are romantic and creative, and what we're looking for in an intimate relationship. Every Venus transit accentuates a different part of our romantic souls. During a Venus transit in a sign that has the same element as your sun sign—water for you, Cancer—the qualities of that element are heightened. You feel more attractive, self-confident, optimistic, enthusiastic. You get the idea. Venus in a water sign makes you feel generally better about life, deepens your emotional flow and your intuition.

Mars symbolizes our physical energy, aggression, sexuality. So when Mars is in a fellow water sign, you're more you—intuitive, subjective, imaginative, nurturing. Sexually, you're ready for a meaningful relationship.

Here are the dates when Mars is in a water sign:

February 1–March 12. During this period Mars is in Pisces, so your imagination is really ramped up. If you can imagine it, Cancer, then it can happen. Your energy should be good during this transit; your sexuality is certainly heightened.

July 13–August 27. Mars transits your sign! This period is when you should really be in your element. Your physical and sexual energy are superb, and you pursue what and who you desire. If you're involved in a relationship already, then things should move along at a pace that suits you. This transit brings your energy and focus to romance, love, creativity. If you and your partner have thought about starting a family, then pregnancy could occur during this transit.

Other Important Dates

We talk about new and full moons elsewhere in the book, but in terms of love, romance, and sex, here are some dates to circle:

March 13. New moon in Pisces. This one should be incredible for you. Six out of ten planets are in Pisces. The emphasis is on intuition, psychic experiences, deep connections with your partner, and all sorts of new opportunities for creative ventures and overseas travel.

July 8. New moon in your sign. This new moon occurs just once a year. It ushers in new personal opportunities that should please you. Plan for it by creating a wish board of your desires. Back your desires with emotion. Post your wish board where you'll see it often. Trust that the universe will make things happen. Five out of ten planets are in your sign during this new moon, including expansive Jupiter. You can do no wrong, Cancer! And even if you do a wrong, people are exceptionally forgiving.

November 3. Solar eclipse in Scorpio. This one is all about romance, love, creativity, and the new opportunities that surface in those areas. It favors all things Scorpionic—investigation, research, psychic phenomena, powerful emotions.

Once Jupiter enters your sign on June 25, you're in for a real treat in all areas of your life. Read more about the Jupiter transit in the Big Picture for your sign.

CHAPTER 14

Your Spirituality in 2013

Neptune is the most mysterious of planets, so far from Earth that Voyager 2 had to travel for twelve years to reach it. Its atmosphere is composed of hydrogen, helium, and frozen methane, which gives Neptune's clouds their blue color. These clouds whip around the planet at speeds of up to 700 miles an hour. The planet's diameter at the equator is almost four times that of Earth. It's nearly seventeen times as massive, but less dense than our planet. Like Pluto, it can't be seen without a telescope.

In astrology this planet represents what is hidden and veiled. At its height it symbolizes illusions and spiritual insights and stimulates imagination, artistic inspiration, flashes of genius, and all that is mystical. It also symbolizes your personal unconscious. On the down side, it represents delusion, escapism, addiction of all kinds, deception. It's the natural ruler of Pisces and the twelfth house. It takes about fourteen years to move through a sign and roughly 168 years to move through the zodiac. Only Pluto moves more slowly. Its impact, then, is felt over time, in subtle ways.

In February 2012 it entered Pisces, the sign it rules, where it will be for the next fourteen years. During this long transit Neptune is in your solar ninth house, forming a beneficial angle to your sun. The ninth house rules your worldview, spiritual beliefs, publishing, higher education, and foreign travel, so these areas will work well for you during the transit. Your spiritual beliefs will deepen, your intuitive ability expand. Your ideals become ever more important to you. You may delve into everything that is hidden, invisible, mysterious, the big cosmic questions. What happens after death? Is it possible to communicate with the dead? What is mediumship? Memories may surface of your past lives.

Many psychic and spiritual experiences will accompany this transit. You may see ghosts or become interested in reincarnation and communication with the dead. You may join a ghost-hunter group or take meditation classes. You may delve into alternative healing, the development of your intuition, you might even take a seminar or workshop in dream recall. Your dreams, in fact, should be quite vivid throughout this transit, and with a little practice you could easily become proficient at recalling them and gleaning insights and information from them.

You may get involved in charity work or could volunteer for an animal shelter, a community center, a homeless shelter. During this transit it's likely that you'll seek friends, coworkers, and groups that are more in alignment with your ideals and spiritual beliefs. There can sometimes be confusion with Neptune transits because this planet blurs the border between self and others. But later in the chapter we'll provide suggestions for mitigating the confusion and getting the most out of this transit.

Dates to Watch For

Between **February 25 and March 21** Venus will be traveling with Neptune, in Pisces. This period favors all kinds of creativity, working with groups, co-workers, bosses. Allow your intuition to guide you, and the transit will be a welcome change. It's super for your love life too, Cancer, with a powerful emotional flow between you and your partner.

On **March 11** the new moon in Pisces will usher in new opportunities to travel abroad, expand your business to overseas markets, or go to college or graduate school. You may take courses or workshops in intuitive development. On the day of that new moon six planets will be in Pisces with Neptune and Mercury traveling very closely together. So around this time you may be discussing or writing about your spiritual beliefs, your travel experiences, or your creative endeavors. You might join an online discussion group or forum concerning spirituality or psychic phenomena. Or you may start blogging about your experiences.

June 6–November 13. Neptune will be retrograde in Pisces. This movement tends to drive your searching inward. You may scrutinize your spiritual beliefs in an effort to define which beliefs are those adopted from family and friends and which beliefs are actually yours.

If you've always had a yearning to write a book, the new moon in Pisces could bring the nudge you need to get started. With Neptune in Pisces, you can easily write from an inspired place within yourself. Neptune rules our higher minds, the part of us that is connected to what Esther and Jerry Hicks call Source energy, to the divine, to the part of us that is larger, vaster, wiser.

Synchronicity and Neptune

Synchronicity, a term coined by Carl Jung, is the coming together of inner and outer events in a way that can't be explained by cause and effect and is meaningful to the observer. Meaningful coincidences. You may experience a lot of these during Neptune's transit through Pisces.

Synchronicities can involve anything. You might be driving along, thinking about a particular person or issue and then hear something on the car radio that seems to address that very individual or issue. These experiences often act as wakeup calls that open you to a greater reality, to the realization that we are all connected, that what affects one affects all. Once you become aware of meaningful coincidences, you'll notice that they often manifest themselves through global events. Then it's as if the universe is addressing us as a collective—as people of the same country, continent, world. The oil spill in the Gulf of Mexico certainly qualifies as a global synchronicity.

On March 31, 2010, President Obama unveiled a sweeping plan to open up the eastern Gulf of Mexico, the south Atlantic coast, and areas off northern Alaska to new oil and gas exploration. As noted in the *St. Petersburg Times,* "Never mind that the eastern gulf has less oil than America consumes in a year. Any supplies would not make a dent in the price of fuel at the pump. But moving the boundary east would shift the next fight over drilling even closer to land."

Just twenty days later, on April 20, a BP oil rig exploded in the gulf, just fifty miles off the Louisiana coast, killing eleven people and creating what has become the worst oil spill in history. On the day of the explosion, BP executives were on the rig, celebrating their safety record. It was as if the universe said, *Safety record? Are you kidding? I don't think so, boys.*

Synchronicities often involve clusters—of numbers, names, objects, virtually anything. A common cluster of numbers involves 11, 111, 11:11. One day, for example, when we were working on a chapter in our book, *7 Secrets of Synchronicity*, we received a bill from our daughter's college for the year-end cleaning of the dorm suite she shared with three other women. The charge was $111 and loose change.

That same day, in the midst of corresponding with people on our blog (http:ofscarabs.blogspot.com), we took a break so Rob could pick up our car from the shop. It had just gotten its second alternator in two weeks. He drove away from the garage at 3:17 P.M. and looked down at the dashboard clock to see if it registered the same time as his watch. But because the battery had been disconnected, the clock had stopped. The time? 11:11.

Jung believed that repeated clusters of a number mean that number has become active in your psyche. So if you experience clusters of numbers—or anything else, for that matter—do some research on it. Clusters of 11s, for instance, tend to occur during periods of heightened awareness. Psychic Uri Geller, who writes extensively about this cluster on his Web site, considers 11:11 to be a doorway, "a crack between two worlds . . . a bridge which has the inherent potential of linking together two very different spirals of energy."

Neptune in Pisces heightens your awareness of underlying patterns, and synchronicity is all about repeating patterns. You may want to keep a journal about your synchronicity experiences. Over time you'll be able to decipher the message of your synchronicities more quickly and accurately. Keep in mind that synchronicities can originate in dreams, usually as precognitive or telepathic information.

Neptune will be retrograde between June 6 and November 13. During this period your inward seeking will be intense.

Suggestions

Even though Neptune in Pisces forms a beneficial angle to your sun, here are some suggestions to keep the confusion at a minimum:

- Check your hunches against the facts.
- Don't allow others to take advantage of you.
- Explore your ideals and how you might integrate them more readily into your life.
- Take classes in intuitive development.
- Learn to recall your dreams, and request information and insights about things that concern you.

- Start meditating. This should be easy for you to do, Cancer. As a water sign, you're attuned to your inner world.
- Establish a regular exercise routine if you don't have one already. Exercise will help to ground you.
- Pay close attention to what you eat. If possible, stick to fresh fruits and vegetables and go organic!

CHAPTER 15

Navigating Saturn in 2013 for Cancer

Saturn offers no free rides. Keep that in mind. Whatever this planet brings into your life, you've worked for it, earned it in this life or another.

The areas that Saturn rules reflect its stern nature. Think of it as a school marm, shaking its finger in your face, reminding you to live up to your responsibilities, be disciplined in what you do, and erect solid, durable structures in your life. Limitations, delays, and restrictions also fall under Saturn's rule. So do teeth and bones. It's known as the planet of karma.

Where it appears in your birth chart is the area where you will learn responsibility. Saturn shows us our limitations, and through it we learn the rules of the game here in physical reality.

This planet takes about two and a half years to transit a sign and about twenty-nine years to move through the zodiac. Each sign, every angle it forms to your sun, teaches you something different. Every twenty-nine years, however, you experience a Saturn return, when the planet returns to where it was when you were born. The first one happens around the age of twenty-nine, the second one when you're between the ages of fifty-eight and sixty, and the third one, if you live long enough, around the age of ninety. These returns are major turning points in life.

At the first Saturn return you get married or divorced, start a family, embark on a career, go to graduate school. You get the idea. These events are major transitions that pivot your life in new directions.

At your second Saturn return the events are no less dramatic, but you're older and more seasoned, in a better place to put them into the larger context of your life. This is when people retire, care for aging parents, become empty-nesters, downsize, and even sometimes start new careers, doing what they love and have postponed for years.

The third Saturn return seems to be one of reflection. It's when you appreciate the life you have lived, forgive yourself and others, find satisfaction in what you have accomplished, and gain a deeper understanding of where you have been, who you are, and where you are going. The third return may also be when, at some level, you begin to plan for your next life.

Saturn in 2013

On October 5, 2012, Saturn left Libra and entered Scorpio, where it will be until December 24, 2014. In mid-June 2015 Saturn will dip back into Scorpio, but in September 2015 it will enter Sagittarius, where it will be until late December 2017.

During Saturn's transit through Scorpio, in your solar fifth house, your love life, creativity, and children will be redefined in a positive way. During this transit it forms a beneficial angle with your sun, strengthening all those attributes that constitute who you are. In romance and love, for instance, you won't settle for a shallow relationship. You're interested in substance, deep intuitive connections, partners who are self-confident. In your creative endeavors you'll be able to find the perfect structures for your projects. Your relationship with your children deepens.

Your intuition should be so greatly enhanced that you and your partner/love interest could experience telepathic moments, when one of you completes what the other was about to say. Your dreams are likely to be profound and vivid, and it would be to your benefit to work with them, seeking patterns of information and precognition. You'll be much more aware of your environment—externally and internally. You may explore divination systems—the I Ching, tarot, even astrology.

Whenever Scorpio is part of the astrological equation, depth is key. Depth in relationships, your daily work, your spiritual beliefs, depth through and through. Intense emotions and psychic experiences are also part of what Scorpio is about. You may be delving more deeply into the unseen side of life, into all that is mysterious—ghosts, hauntings, orbs, synchronicities that involve dreams, communication with the dead, precognitive information, memories of past lives. Or you may undertake that exploration with a coworker, friend, or partner.

Good books for this transit? Anything by author Jane Roberts, who for years channeled Seth, "a personality essence no longer focused in physical existence." The twenty or so books that Roberts channeled covered the gamut of esoteric topics. Other recommendations: *The Holographic Universe* by Michael Talbot, anything by Esther and Jerry Hicks, *Children's Past Lives* by Carol Bowman.

Dates to Watch For

April 25. Lunar eclipse in Scorpio. Your love life races like a furious river. Passions run high. Transformation is afoot. Saturn is close to this eclipse degree, suggesting a seriousness to any news you hear.

June 25, 2013–July 16, 2014. Jupiter transits your sign, Cancer, and with it comes all sorts of wonderful stuff. Jupiter expands everything it touches and makes sure you're in the right place at the right time, meeting the right people, landing the right job. You're in the flow, you tap into your creativity, your personal life expands in some way. Look at your natal chart to find out where Cancer falls. If it's in your tenth house, then Jupiter will bring new career options and opportunities. If it's in your second, then look for an expansion in your finances.

During this period Jupiter forms a beneficial angle to Saturn in Scorpio, which is the equivalent of having your birthday and Christmas last all year.

November 3. The solar eclipse in Scorpio features five planets in this sign, including Saturn. This one is apt to be intense and powerful for you and your love life, creativity, and relationship with your kids. If you don't have children, then the eclipse may change that! It's an ideal time to start a family.

June 2–27. Venus transits your sign, Cancer, forms a beneficial angle to Saturn, and for a couple of days travels with Jupiter. This period marks one of the most romantic and creative times for you all year. Make good use of the energy!

July 13–August 27. Mars transits Cancer, travels with Jupiter, and acts as an intuitive booster rocket. Your physical and sexual energy during this period is excellent. You're in a powerful place.

Meaningful relationships will become a priority when Venus travels with Saturn between **September 11 and October 7.** This period brings a serious tone and texture to any business or romantic partnerships. You and your partner may discover such a deep connection that you take your relationship to the next level. Or, equally possible, you discover the darker sides of Scorpio—envy, jealousy, possessiveness, manipulation—and decide to end things.

Between **September 29 and October 21** Mercury, planet of communication and travel, joins Saturn in Scorpio. This transit brings greater depth to your conscious mind. You are more intuitive, perhaps more secretive, but are looking for the absolute bottom line in everything you do, feel, investigate, and think. You will expect complete honesty in all your dealings with people. Be prepared to offer the same.

- Establish a schedule for your creative work. Stick to it. During your creativity time, let your imagination wander freely.
- Establish a regular exercise regimen. Join a gym, take up yoga.
- Meditate.

- Explore your feelings, and be willing to communicate what you feel.
- Be alert for synchronicities—meaningful coincidences. These synchronicities can be guide posts, signs along the path of your life that point you in a particular direction. They can act as confirmation, warning, reassurance.
- Ask for guidance in your dreams—Neptune in Pisces should help in that regard.
- Take a workshop in intuitive development, alternative healing, or in something creative that interests you.
- Read, read, read.
- Start a blog.
- Create a space in your home to which you can retreat when you feel overwhelmed.
- Be conscious about your nutrition—conscious, not obsessive.
- Pat yourself on the back whenever you do something well!
- Practice appreciating everything in your environment.

CHAPTER 16

Using Pluto to Your Advantage in 2013

Pluto entered Capricorn in 2008, about the same time that Wall Street began to collapse, the housing market tanked, and the economy turned south. That's also when it began its opposition to your sun. More on that in a moment. Let's take a deeper look at what Pluto is about.

Pluto lost its status as a planet on August 24, 2006. On that day the International Astronomical Union voted to demote Pluto to a dwarf planet. It apparently doesn't meet the three conditions necessary for a celestial body to be considered a planet:

- The body must orbit a star.
- It must be massive enough for its own gravity to pull it into a nearly spherical shape.
- The object has "cleared the neighborhood" around its orbit.

Pluto meets the first two criteria. The third criterion is where Pluto failed. According to infoplease .com, ". . . the other planets have either assimilated or repulsed most other objects in their orbits, and each has more mass than the combined total of everything else in its area." Pluto is just one of numerous objects in its orbit.

However, to astrologers, it remains a potent force in the zodiac. Discovered in 1930, Pluto is the most distant planet from the sun. It exists at the edge of the solar system, its light so dim it seems etheric. It takes 248 years to make a circuit of the zodiac, i.e., it moves like a snail. But this slow movement is what makes its transits so powerful—at least to astrologers!

This small, powerful celestial body represents profound, irrevocable transformation. When it entered Capricorn in 2008, it began to bring about change from the bottom up in government, authority figures, and corporate entities that are "too big to fail" and started exposing the dark underbelly of corruption and greed.

Pluto's last transit through Capricorn occurred between November 1762 and December 1, 1778. Let's take a closer look at what was going on then:

- Unrest and outright rebellion and revolution were evident during much of this period in Europe and the colonies.
- Spain acquired Louisiana from France.
- Catherine the Great became empress and presided over wars with the Ottoman Empire.
- Britain struck a deal with Spain to exchange Cuba for Florida.
- The first partition of Poland happened during this period, when that country was divided into three areas owned by Russia, Prussia, and Austria.

- The Quartering Act was passed, requiring the housing of British troops in private homes.
- Parliament passed the Stamp Act, its first serious attempt to assert governmental authority over the colonies. It was intended to pay for the huge national debt Britain had incurred during the Seven Years War, but created a serious threat of revolt.
- The Boston Tea Party occurred during Pluto's last passage through Capricorn.

In other words dramatic, transformative events occurred, just as they are now. But before you panic, Cancer, let's take a closer look at how your life may be impacted and the control you have to turn the tide, if necessary.

Since 2008 Pluto has been moving through your solar seventh house, forming an opposition to your sun. This transit affects everything associated with your partnerships—business and romantic—and with your career goals, the Capricorn part of the equation. An opposition is challenging. It creates an axis of tension in your life that you simply have to move through. You can't allow it to undermine your life. We'll look at some suggestions later in the chapter for maintaining your self-confidence and direction.

Look at your natal chart to find where Capricorn falls. That's where the greatest transformation will occur. If Capricorn is on the cusp of your second house, then your finances will undergo change. If it's on the cusp of your fourth house, then your home life will undergo change. The transit lasts until 2024.

Important dates to remember:

April 12–September 20. Pluto is moving retrograde during this period. It means that certain things aren't moving ahead as swiftly as you would like. You may be scrutinizing your deeper goals for 2013, reworking your partnership needs.

November 5, 2013–February 6, 2014. Venus travels with Pluto during this period. The planet's transit usually lasts about three weeks, but it will be retrograde between **December 21 and January 30**. When Venus is moving direct, it may attract a special person into your life, someone you meet through your business or career, perhaps. If something develops with a coworker, think twice about getting deeply involved.

December 24, 2013–January 12, 2014. Mercury will be in Capricorn, traveling for a time with both Pluto and Venus. This trio brings deep discussions about partnership issues and the vision you and your partner have about your relationship.

Jupiter enters Cancer on **June 25** and will be opposed to Pluto for part of July. Between **July 1 and 21** the opposition could exacerbate tension in some area of your life. You may be prone to blowing things out of proportion and making hasty decisions based on insufficient information. Your emotions will be quite powerful during this period.

January 11 features a new moon in Capricorn with Mercury closely conjunct and Pluto closely conjunct to Mercury but not to the new moon. Still, because Pluto is involved, any new opportunities that surface are likely to be deeply transformative. Consider them carefully.

Since Pluto in Capricorn forms a challenging angle to your sun, here are some suggestions to make its energy work in your favor:

- Make adjustments in your life when necessary. You're one of the most flexible signs and can easily adjust when you should.
- Take time out daily just for yourself. Whether you nap, read a book, drive around, visit friends, shop, or go to the gym, do whatever brings *you* pleasure.
- Establish a regular exercise routine if you don't have one already. As a Cancer, you benefit from whatever helps you deal with your emotions.
- Start meditating. This shouldn't be a problem for you, Cancer. Start small, a few minutes a day. You may surprise yourself and realize that you enjoy it.
- Practice dream recall. Your dreams are great sources of information and insight. Give yourself a suggestion before falling asleep that you'll wake up after an important dream and be able to remember it. Keep your dream journal handy.
- Be mindful of what you eat. Notice the ingredients. Is the item high in sodium? Fats? Cut out red meats. Go organic when possible.
- Take a seminar or workshop in intuitive development or some other topic that interests you.
- Start a novel or log. Your communication skills are always excellent.

Pluto transits, by their very nature, are intense no matter what sign they're in. Once you've found where Capricorn falls in your natal chart, then reread the Houses section in chapter 2 to understand which area of your life will be impacted.

CHAPTER 17

The Big Picture for Cancer in 2013

Welcome to 2013! And what a year it's going to be for you, Cancer, with surprises and luck coming at you from every side. It's your year to lead, forge new paths into the unknown, break free of any ruts and routines that may have dragged you down in 2012.

We've covered some of the major transits that will be happening this year and how they'll affect you. So let's look at the inner planets, those that move more swiftly, and see what effects they may have on your life.

Romance/Creativity

Your solar fifth house is Scorpio. This means that any time an inner planet transits that house, things heat up romantically, creatively, with your kids. Your enjoyment becomes paramount. These transits always form beneficial angles to your sun, so it's easier for you to be you!

There are several periods this year when romance

and creativity really flow your way. Between June 2 and 27 Venus transits your sign. This period is remarkably charged with everything that makes you happy. Your self-confidence soars; others find you enormously appealing and intriguing. Romance, love, and creative endeavors are high on your list of priorities. You may be in love with love, Cancer, which is a good thing, as long as you don't allow it to color the facts.

Between September 11 and October 7 Venus transits Scorpio, your solar fifth house, making this the most romantic and creative period for you all year. If you aren't involved when the transit begins, you probably will be by the time it ends. If you're in a relationship, things between you and your partner simply get better. You may even work together on a creative project. Your muse is at your beck and call 24/7, so take advantage of it!

From February 25 to March 21 Venus moves through fellow water sign Pisces, your solar ninth house. This period should be another good one. You and your partner may hit the road—foreign or domestic—and you should have the bigger picture of what the relationship is really all about. It's a good period for creative endeavors too, because your imagination is as big as Texas.

Career

In addition to the dates mentioned in chapter 15, there are some other stellar dates for professional matters this year. When Venus transits Aries and your career area between March 21 and April 15, it's time to ask for a raise or promotion, pitch ideas, and garner support for a project. There's a certain professional ease with this transit that prompts others to see you as the person with the answers or with the wisdom and skills to lead others. Venus in Aries enables you to more actively seek what you desire professionally. You're fearless.

Good backup dates? Between April 13 and May 1, Mercury transits Aries and your career area, an excellent time to discuss and pitch your ideas. You may be hanging out with people from work. You have a clear sense about what you're doing. You're excellent at starting things during this period, but leave the completion to someone else.

Finances

If you have been struck by the downturn in the economy that began in 2008, your financial picture probably will improve considerably this year. Between June 25, 2013, and July 15, 2014, expansive Jupiter transits your sign. This period should be magnificent for you, with many new personal opportunities and new ideas that enable you to find exactly what you need, before you need it! The period between January 1 and June 25 should be good, too, when Jupiter in Gemini forms a beneficial angle with your career area. This transit could bring about a promotion, raise, career or job change.

While Jupiter is in your sign, you're able to make money by following your intuitive guidance. Don't let facts cloud your vision of what is possible. Your dreams should be a great resource for insight and information, so learn to work with them, recall them, request information through them.

Mercury Retrogrades

Every year Mercury—the planet of communication and travel—turns retrograde three times. During these periods it's wise not to sign contracts (unless you don't mind renegotiating when Mercury is moving direct), to check and recheck travel plans, and to communicate as succinctly as possible. Refrain from buying any large-ticket items or electronics during this time too. Often computers and appliances go on the fritz, cars act up, data is lost . . . you get the idea. Be sure to back up all files before the dates below:

February 23–March 17: Mercury retrograde in Pisces, your solar ninth house. This one could mess up your travel plans or toss a wrench into anything that revolves around publishing, education, or foreign business interests.

June 26–July 20: Mercury retrograde in your sign. This one could be challenging. Be sure to meditate more frequently during this period. Take up yoga so that you maintain your flexibility—physically and emotionally. Breathe through the snafus.

October 21–November 10: Mercury retrograde in Scorpio, your solar fifth house. It impacts your love life, creativity, your kids. Communicate clearly. Lots of psychological stuff could surface—that's the Scorpio part of the equation.

Eclipses

Solar eclipses tend to trigger external events that bring about change according to the sign and house in which they fall. Lunar eclipses trigger inner, emotional events according to the sign and house in which they fall. Any eclipse marks both beginnings and endings. The solar and lunar eclipse in a pair falls in opposite signs. If you're interested in detailed information on eclipses, take a look at Celeste Teal's excellent and definitive book, *Eclipses: Predicting World Events & Personal Transformation.*

If you were born under or around the time of an eclipse, it's to your advantage to take a look at your birth chart to find out exactly where the eclipses will impact you.

Most years feature four eclipses—two solar, two lunar—with the set separated by about two weeks. This year there are three lunar eclipses and two solar eclipses. Let's take a closer look.

April 25: Lunar eclipse in Scorpio. This one should bring news related to your love life and creative endeavors. Emotions are stirred up. Time to research and investigate.

May 9: Solar eclipse in Taurus. This eclipse should usher in new opportunities to make friends, join groups, and to realize your wishes and dreams. You may have to relinquish something before you can take advantage of the opportunities. Should be positive for you!

May 25: Lunar eclipse in Sagittarius, your solar sixth house. This eclipse brings news about a daily work matter or about your health. There could also be news about a publishing project, foreign travel, or educational matters.

October 18: Lunar eclipse in Aries, in your career area. This one brings news and stirs emotions concerning professional matters and relationships. Venus forms a strong angle to the eclipse degree, however, so it looks as if news that you hear is positive.

November 3: Solar eclipse in Scorpio, your solar fifth house. This one triggers external events related to everything discussed under the April 25 lunar eclipse. Four planets and the North Node are in Scorpio during this eclipse, so get ready for intensity and power.

Luckiest Day of the Year

Every year there's one day when Jupiter and the sun meet up, and luck, serendipity, and expansion are the hallmarks. This year that day falls on June 19, in Gemini. A stellar day!

CHAPTER 18

Eighteen Months of Day-by-Day Predictions: July 2012 to December 2013

Moon sign times are calculated for Eastern Standard Time and Eastern Daylight Time. Please adjust for your local time zone.

JULY 2012

Sunday, July 1 (Moon in Sagittarius)   The moon is in your sixth house today. It's a service day. Visit someone who is ill or in need of your assistance. Help others, but avoid falling into a martyr syndrome. You could feel somewhat emotionally repressed now. It's a good day to clarify any health or work issues.

Monday, July 2 (Moon into Capricorn, 6:52 p.m.) Look beyond the immediate. Clear up odds and ends. Take an inventory on where things are going in your life. The old cycle is ending; a new one about to begin. Accept what comes your way today; it's all part of a cycle.

Tuesday, July 3 (Moon in Capricorn)   Mars moves into your fourth house today, suggesting aggressiveness in your home environment for the next few weeks. Arguments could erupt with family members. You might be actively involved in a home-repair project. There's also a full moon in your seventh house today, and that means you reap what you've sown related to partnerships. You gain a better understanding of a partner.

Wednesday, July 4 (Moon into Aquarius, 8:26 p.m.) Use your intuition to get a sense of the day. A partnership plays an important role. Be kind and understanding. Don't make waves. Just flow with the current; accept what comes your way.

Thursday, July 5 (Moon in Aquarius)   The moon in your eighth house can affect your feelings about your possessions, as well as things that you share with others, such as a spouse. Your experiences are more intense than usual. It's a good day to explore a metaphysical subject, such as life after death or the meaning of dreams.

Friday, July 6 (Moon in Aquarius)   You have deeper contact with friends now. Scorpio and Pisces play a role. You join a group of like-minded individuals. Social consciousness plays a role. Your sense of security is tied to your relationships and friends.

Saturday, July 7 (Moon into Pisces, 12:29 a.m.) Promote new ideas now; follow your curiosity. Freedom of thought and action is key. Think outside the box. Take risks; experiment. Variety is the spice of life.

Sunday, July 8 (Moon in Pisces)   The moon is in your ninth house today, the home of higher education and long-distance travel. You're full of ideas on matters such as philosophy or religion, the law or publishing. You also have a strong interest in foreign travel or a foreign nation.

Monday, July 9 (Moon into Aries, 8:14 a.m.)   It's a number 7 day, your mystery day. You launch a journey into the unknown. Secrets, intrigue, confidential information play a role. Make sure that you see things as they are, not as you wish them to be. Express your desires, but avoid self-deception. Maintain your emotional balance.

Tuesday, July 10 (Moon in Aries)   The moon is in your tenth house today. You're feeling ambitious, pushing ahead in your career. You've got your eye on a promotion, but make sure you attend to details, Cancer. It's a good day for sales and dealing with the public and coworkers. You're aiming high, shooting for the moon, so to speak.

Wednesday, July 11 (Moon into Taurus, 7:30 p.m.) Finish what you started. Visualize the future; set your goals, then make them so. Clear up odds and ends. Take an inventory on where things are going in your life. It's a good day to make a donation to a worthy cause.

Thursday, July 12 (Moon in Taurus)   The moon is in your eleventh house today. You work well with others, especially in a group. Friends play a surprisingly important role, especially Scorpio and Cancer. Focus on your wishes and dreams. Examine your overall goals, and make sure that they're still an expression of who you are.

Friday, July 13 (Moon in Taurus)   Uranus goes retrograde in your tenth house today and stays there until December 13. You could experience some delays related to any interest in getting a promotion or raise. Expect some erratic behavior by people around you, if not your own actions. You could have some difficulty making up your mind. Everything seems somewhat uncertain, and your coworkers aren't necessarily offering you the best advice.

Saturday, July 14 (Moon into Gemini, 8:27 a.m.) Mercury goes retrograde in your second house today and stays there until August 8. That means there could be some miscommunication over the next three weeks related to finances. There could be delays and confusion related to what's owed to you or what you owe. There could also be communication glitches with cell phones or e-mail. Think carefully before making any major purchases while Mercury remains retrograde.

Sunday, July 15 (Moon in Gemini)   The moon is in your twelfth house today. It's best to remain behind the scenes and avoid public scrutiny. Unconscious attitudes can be difficult today and could relate to the past and your childhood. It's a good day to pursue a spiritual or mystical discipline.

Monday, July 16 (Moon into Cancer, 8:32 p.m.) It's a number 5 day. That means change and variety are highlighted. Think freedom, no restrictions. You're seeking new horizons, new possibilities. Promote new ideas; follow your curiosity. Look for adventure. Freedom of thought and action is key.

Tuesday, July 17 (Moon in Cancer)   The moon is in your first house today, Cancer. Your self-awareness and appearance are important now. You're dealing with your emotional self, the person you are becoming. You might feel moody—happy one moment, sad or withdrawn the next. However, your thoughts and feelings are aligned. You tend to search for ways to improve yourself.

Wednesday, July 18 (Moon in Cancer)   With the moon on your ascendant, you're more appealing to others. Your face is in front of the public. The way you see yourself now is the way others see you. You're physically vital, and relations with the opposite sex go well.

Thursday, July 19 (Moon into Leo, 6:14 a.m.) There's a new moon in your first house, so you're recharged for the rest of the month and beyond, and this makes you more appealing to a love interest. New opportunities come your way, and they expand your possibilities.

Friday, July 20 (Moon in Leo)   With the moon in your second house today, money and material goods are important to you and give you a sense of security. You identify emotionally with your possessions or whatever you value. Watch your spending, and collect what's owed to you.

Saturday, July 21 (Moon into Virgo, 1:25 p.m.)
It's a number 1 day, and you're at the top of your cycle, Cancer. Trust your hunches today. You get a fresh start, a new beginning. You're inventive and make connections that others overlook. Get out and meet new people, have new experiences, do something you've never done before.

Sunday, July 22 (Moon in Virgo) The moon is in your third house today. Take what you know and share it with others. You get your ideas across now, but you need to control your emotions. Your thinking is unduly influenced by things of the past. Relatives and neighbors could play a role in your day.

Monday, July 23 (Moon into Libra, 6:39 p.m.) It's a number 3 day, and everything eases up now. The intensity you've been feeling evaporates. Be happy, positive, upbeat. Your attitude determines everything. You're well liked and receive a social invitation. Your charm and wit are appreciated. Spend time in conversation. Hobbies are accented.

Tuesday, July 24 (Moon in Libra) The moon is in your fourth house today. Spend time with your family and loved ones. You get along better now with them. Stick close to home, if possible. A parent plays a role in your day. You're dealing with the foundations of who you are and who you are becoming.

Wednesday, July 25 (Moon into Scorpio, 10:30 p.m.)
Freedom of thought and action are highlighted.
Change your perspective. Approach the day with an
unconventional mind-set. You can overcome obstacles with ease. It's a good day to pursue self-
employment. You're courageous and adaptable.

Thursday, July 26 (Moon in Scorpio)   The moon
is in your fifth house today. Your emotions tend to
overpower your intellect. You feel strongly attached
to loved ones, particularly children. But eventually
you need to let go. Your creativity is highlighted.

Friday, July 27 (Moon in Scorpio)   Expect intense,
emotional experiences today. You're passionate, and
your sexuality is heightened. Be aware of things happening in secret and of possible deception. Control issues might arise. Forgive and forget; try to avoid going
to extremes.

Saturday, July 28 (Moon into Sagittarius, 1:18 a.m.)
It's your power day and your day to play it your way.
You can go far with your plans and achieve financial
success, especially if you open your mind to a new approach. It's a good day to buy a lotto ticket.

Sunday, July 29 (Moon in Sagittarius)   The moon
is in your sixth house today. It's a service day. Others
rely on you now. You're the one they go to for answers. Help them, but don't deny your own needs.
Keep your resolutions about exercise, and watch your
diet.

Monday, July 30 (Moon into Capricorn, 3:30 a.m.) You're at the top of your cycle today. Trust your hunches; intuition is highlighted. You're inventive and make connections that others overlook. Refuse to deal with people who have closed minds. In romance, something new is developing.

Tuesday, July 31 (Moon in Capricorn)   With the moon in your seventh house today, your relationship with a lover or partner is highlighted. Women play a prominent role in your day. You feel a need to be accepted. You're looking for security, but you have a hard time going with the flow. A legal matter comes to a head now.

AUGUST 2012

Wednesday, August 1 (Moon into Aquarius, 5:56 a.m.)   There's a full moon in your eighth house today. You gain illumination and insight related to property or resources that you share with someone, such as a spouse. Also, you see a metaphysical subject in a new light. Be alert for issues related to taxes, a mortgage, insurance, or investments. Go with the flow.

Thursday, August 2 (Moon in Aquarius)   The moon is in your eighth house today. You're somewhat moody now, and things could get contentious in your dealings with someone of the opposite sex. That's particularly true if you're facing issues related to shared belongings. You're also intuitive, and you could take a renewed interest in past lives, astrology, or life after death.

Friday, August 3 (Moon into Pisces, 9:58 a.m.)
Your intuition focuses on relationships now. Be kind and understanding. Don't make waves. Don't rush or show resentment; let things develop. Marriage or a partnership plays a key role in your day. Take time again today to consider the direction you're headed and your motivation for continuing on this path.

Saturday, August 4 (Moon in Pisces)   The moon is in your ninth house today, Cancer. You're a dreamer and a thinker. You're captivated by new ideas and philosophies. You may feel a need to get away now, a break from the usual routine. You're feeling free, but also restless and yearning for a new experience.

Sunday, August 5 (Moon into Aries, 4:59 p.m.)
Your organizational skills are highlighted now, but try not to wander off task. Take care of details. Emphasize quality. You're seeking perfection, building a creative foundation for your future. Tear down the old in order to rebuild. Be methodical and thorough.

Monday, August 6 (Moon in Aries)   The moon is in your tenth house today. You're thinking about domestic matters, Cancer, and you could be exchanging ideas about your home with friends and associates. You also take part in a group activity, and others are impressed with your passion, especially if you're working for the common good. Follow your wishes and dreams.

Tuesday, August 7 (Moon in Aries)   Venus moves into your first house today. Your personal grace and charm are emphasized. You're more self-confident and appealing to the opposite sex. It's a good month for a love affair to develop.

Wednesday, August 8 (Moon into Taurus, 3:28 a.m.)
Mercury goes direct today in your second house. That means any confusion, miscommunication, and delays related to finances and money matters that you've experienced in recent weeks recede into the past. Things move more smoothly now. That's especially true related to your higher-education plans or intention to take a long trip. Everything works better, including computers and other electronic equipment.

Thursday, August 9 (Moon in Taurus) The moon is in your eleventh house today. Friends play an important role in your day. Focus on your wishes and dreams. Examine your overall goals, and make sure that those goals are an expression of who you are. Your sense of security is tied to your relationships and friends.

Friday, August 10 (Moon into Gemini, 4:12 p.m.)
It's a number 9 day, a great time to finish whatever you've been working on. Clear up odds and ends. Make room for something new, but don't start anything until tomorrow. Look beyond the immediate. Take an inventory on where things are going in your life.

Saturday, August 11 (Moon in Gemini) With the moon in your twelfth house, it's a good day to withdraw and spend time in private. Relax and meditate.

Keep your feelings to yourself, unless you confide in a close friend. Follow your intuition. It's a great day for a mystical or spiritual discipline.

Sunday, August 12 (Moon in Gemini)   You're feeling restless and looking for something fun to do. Your mind moves quickly now from one thought to another. You might not want to spend much time with other people today, but you're certainly thinking about them. It's a good day to settle into a bookstore with a book, a cup of coffee, and maybe your notebook computer.

Monday, August 13 (Moon into Cancer, 4:29 a.m.) It's a number 3 day, and that means you're coming out of your shell. You communicate well. Your attitude determines everything today. Spread your good news. Ease up on routines. Your charm and wit are appreciated. Play your hunches. But also take time to relax and recharge your batteries.

Tuesday, August 14 (Moon in Cancer)   With the moon on your ascendant today, you're physically vital, and relations with the opposite sex go well. You're appealing to the public. Your feelings and thoughts are aligned. Your appearance and personality shine.

Wednesday, August 15 (Moon into Leo, 2:06 p.m.) Variety is the spice of life today. Think outside the box. Take risks; experiment. Let go of old structures; get a new point of view. You're versatile and changeable, but be careful not to spread yourself too thin.

Thursday, August 16 (Moon in Leo)   Expect emotional experiences related to money. Drama is highlighted. You're creative and passionate today, impulsive and honest. You identify emotionally with your possessions or whatever you value. Put off making any major purchases now.

Friday, August 17 (Moon into Virgo, 8:34 p.m.) There's a new moon in your second house today. A new opportunity appears related to your finances. You may be dealing with payments and collecting what's owed to you. You equate your financial assets with emotional security. Look at your priorities in handling your income.

Saturday, August 18 (Moon in Virgo)   The moon is in your third house today. Your mind is occupied with new information, and you're ready to share what you know. However, keep conscious control of your emotions when communicating. Your thinking is unduly influenced by things of the past. A short trip works to your benefit now.

Sunday, August 19 (Moon in Virgo)   Take care of details, especially related to your health. Remember to exercise and watch your diet. Stop worrying and fretting. Stick close to home, focus on tidying up the house, and attend to loose ends. Take time to write in a journal. You write from a deep place now with lots of details and colorful descriptions.

Monday, August 20 (Moon into Libra, 12:46 a.m.) You start out the work week on the top of your cycle.

Get out and meet new people, have new experiences, do something you've never done before. Refuse to deal with people who have closed minds. It's a great day to start a new project. In romance, make room for a new love, if that's what you want. A flirtation turns more serious.

Tuesday, August 21 (Moon in Libra)   The moon is in your fourth house today. It's a good day to work at home, if possible, and also tend to domestic duties, Cancer. That could involve working on a home-repair project or tending to loved ones, especially if you've ignored them recently. Try to avoid getting overly emotional. Spend some time by yourself in quiet meditation.

Wednesday, August 22 (Moon into Scorpio, 3:54 a.m.)   Think positive, stay optimistic. Others look to you for inspiration. You can influence people now with your upbeat attitude. In business dealings, diversify. Insist on all the information, not just bits and pieces.

Thursday, August 23 (Moon in Scorpio)   Mars moves into your fifth house today. It's time to take action regarding a creative project or romance. There's greater emotional depth in whatever you're pursuing. You're aggressive and willing to take a chance. However, you could be overly possessive with loved ones. Be careful about getting into arguments over the next three weeks.

Friday, August 24 (Moon into Sagittarius, 6:50 a.m.)
Variety is the spice of life today. Expect change. Take

a risk; experiment. Alter your perspective, and promote new ideas. You're versatile and changeable, as well as aggressive, but be careful not to spread yourself too thin.

Saturday, August 25 (Moon in Sagittarius)   The moon is in your sixth house. It's a service day. You're the one others go to for help. You improve, edit, or refine their work. Make a doctor or dentist appointment. Your personal health occupies your attention now. Help others, but don't deny your own needs.

Sunday, August 26 (Moon into Capricorn, 9:59 a.m.) It's a number 7 day. Secrets, intrigue, confidential information play a role. You investigate, analyze, or simply observe what's going on now. You quickly come to a conclusion and wonder why others don't see what you see. You detect deception and recognize insincerity with ease. Knowledge is essential to success.

Monday, August 27 (Moon in Capricorn)   The moon is in your seventh house today. You get along well with others now. You can fit in just about anywhere. Loved ones and partners are more important than usual. You focus on how the public relates to you. You feel a need to be accepted. You're looking for security, but you have a hard time going with the flow.

Tuesday, August 28 (Moon into Aquarius, 1:39 p.m.) It's a number 9 day. Visualize the future; set your goals, then make them so. You'll probably find that old ways have outlived their usefulness. Look for a new approach, a new perspective.

Wednesday, August 29 (Moon in Aquarius)   You have a strong sense of duty and feel obligated to fulfill your promises. Your experiences are more intense than usual. Matters relating to sex, death, and rebirth could arise. You investigate a mystery of the unknown, such as past lives or life after death.

Thursday, August 30 (Moon into Pisces, 6:32 p.m.) Cooperation and partnerships are highlighted. You're diplomatic and capable of fixing whatever has gone wrong, especially in the home, Cancer. You're playing the role of the visionary today. Be honest and open.

Friday, August 31 (Moon in Pisces)   Mercury moves into your third house today. That means you express yourself well, especially with relatives or neighbors. Matters related to the past are on your mind. It's a good day to attend a social event. Meanwhile, there's a full moon in your ninth house. You're a dreamer and a thinker. You may feel a need to get away now, a break from the usual routine. Pursuing higher education or long-distance travel is on your mind.

SEPTEMBER 2012

Saturday, September 1 (Moon in Pisces)   You yearn for a new experience. Plan a long trip. Sign up for a workshop or seminar. Any publishing project takes a positive turn today. It's a great time to improve your skills with a foreign language.

Sunday, September 2 (Moon into Aries, 1:38 a.m.) Partnerships are highlighted; cooperation is emphasized. Your intuition focuses on relationships. Don't make waves. Don't rush or show resentment; let things develop. You excel in working with others now. You're playing the role of the visionary today.

Monday, September 3 (Moon in Aries) Professional concerns are the focus of the day. You're looking for an advancement, some recognition, maybe a raise. You're more responsive to the needs and moods of a group and of the public in general. It's a good day for sales, dealing with the public. However, avoid emotional displays.

Tuesday, September 4 (Moon into Taurus, 11:42 a.m.) Your nose goes to the proverbial grindstone today! Hard work is called for. So are your organizational skills. Tear down the old in order to rebuild. Be methodical and thorough. Persevere to get things done, and try to stay focused. It's not a particularly good day to pursue romance. Hold off until tomorrow.

Wednesday, September 5 (Moon in Taurus) Friends play an important role today. You have deeper contact with them now. You join a group of like-minded individuals. You find strength in numbers and meaning through friends and groups. Focus on your wishes and dreams, and make sure that they remain an expression of who you really are.

Thursday, September 6 (Moon in Taurus) With Venus moving into your second house, you could attract a handsome sum of money, and it could relate to an artistic endeavor. You love to surround yourself with your material goods. It's not the objects themselves that are important, but the warm feelings and memories they generate.

Friday, September 7 (Moon into Gemini, 12:11 a.m.) You launch a journey into the unknown today. Secrets, intrigue, confidential information play a role. Make sure that you see things as they are, not as you wish them to be. Express your desires, but avoid self-deception. Maintain your emotional balance.

Saturday, September 8 (Moon in Gemini)   The moon is in your twelfth house today. Unconscious attitudes can be difficult. Keep your feelings secret. You might feel a need to withdraw and work on your own. Take time to reflect and meditate. It's a great time for pursuing a spiritual discipline.

Sunday, September 9 (Moon into Cancer, 12:50 p.m.) Complete a project now. Clear up odds and ends, and make room for something new. Take an inventory on where things are going in your life. Accept what comes your way, but don't start anything. It's all part of a cycle. It's a good day to make a donation to a worthy cause.

Monday, September 10 (Moon in Cancer)   The moon is on your ascendant. The way you see yourself now is the way others see you. You're recharged for the remainder of the month, and this makes you more appealing to the public. You're physically vital, and relations with the opposite sex go well. It's a great day for romance as long as your partner is willing to listen to you talk about your feelings.

Tuesday, September 11 (Moon into Leo, 11:01 p.m.) You could be undergoing some soul-searching related to a relationship. Help comes through friends, loved ones, especially a partner. Don't make waves. Don't rush or show resentment. Let things develop. The spotlight is on cooperation.

Wednesday, September 12 (Moon in Leo) The moon is in your second house today. That means it's a money day. Expect emotional experiences related to finances. Your possessions are meaningful to you now. It's not the objects themselves, but the feelings and memories related to them. Whatever you value most plays a role. Watch your spending.

Thursday, September 13 (Moon in Leo) Romance feels majestic today. Dress boldly; showmanship is emphasized. Strut your stuff. Drama is highlighted, perhaps involving children. Animals or pets play a role in your day.

Friday, September 14 (Moon into Virgo, 5:31 a.m.) Freedom of thought and action is highlighted. Change your perspective, Cancer. Approach the day with an unconventional mind-set. Promote new ideas; follow your curiosity. You can overcome obstacles with ease.

Saturday, September 15 (Moon in Virgo) There's a new moon in your third house today. Watch for new opportunities that appear during your everyday activities. A doorway opens. Take what you know and share it with others. You get your ideas across now, but you need to control your emotions.

Sunday, September 16 (Moon into Libra, 8:55 a.m.) Mercury moves into your fourth house, your native home, Cancer. That means there's lots of energy in the home. If you have children, their friends are coming over, and your day gets somewhat hectic. There's lots of communication in the home, and you could be working there today, possibly on a home-improvement project.

Monday, September 17 (Moon in Libra) With Pluto going direct in your seventh house, your business and personal partnerships will be changing at a profound level. But don't expect immediate changes as you consider a relationship now that is complex and deep. Your partner is strong willed, and you could face some conflicts.

Tuesday, September 18 (Moon into Scorpio, 10:46 a.m.) Finish what you started. Look beyond the immediate. Visualize the future; set your goals, then make them so. Clear your desk, and get ready for a new beginning. But don't start anything today.

Wednesday, September 19 (Moon in Scorpio) It's a great day for pursuing a creative project or a romance. There's greater emotional depth in whatever you pursue. Be yourself; be emotionally honest. Children and animals play a role. Your emotions tend to overpower your intellect now.

Thursday, September 20 (Moon into Sagittarius, 12:34 p.m.)   The spotlight is on cooperation and partnership. Use your intuition to focus on a relationship. Some soul-searching could be called for. Don't make waves. Don't rush or show resentment; let things develop. Your emotions and sensitivity are highlighted.

Friday, September 21 (Moon in Sagittarius)   The moon is in your sixth house today. Your health occupies your attention now. Keep your resolutions about exercise, and watch your diet. Attend to details related to your health. Make a doctor or dentist appointment.

Saturday, September 22 (Moon into Capricorn, 3:21 p.m.)   Hard work is called for now. You make use of your organizational skills. Be methodical and thorough. Persevere to get things done. You're building foundations, establishing a creative base.

Sunday, September 23 (Moon in Capricorn)   Your ambition and drive to succeed are highlighted. Your responsibilities increase. You may feel stressed, overworked today. Don't ignore your exercise routine. Be conservative; don't speculate or take any unnecessary risks.

Monday, September 24 (Moon into Aquarius, 7:33 p.m.)   Think about how you can help others. It's a service day. Be diplomatic in dealing with others. Domestic purchases are highlighted. Some change or adjustment in the home scene works out for the best. Be generous and tolerant.

Tuesday, September 25 (Moon in Aquarius)   The moon is in your eighth house today. Your experiences are more intense and can affect your attitudes toward things you possess or share with others. You have a strong sense of duty and feel obligated to fulfill your promises. Security is an important issue with you right now. You could find yourself managing or controlling the assets of another person. Alternately, you could be dealing with a mystery of the unknown, such as life after death.

Wednesday, September 26 (Moon in Aquarius) You have a greater sense of freedom now. You're dealing with new ideas, new options, originality. You get a new perspective. Play your hunches. Look beyond the immediate; bust old paradigms. Help others, but dance to your own tune. Your wishes and dreams come true. Your individuality is stressed.

Thursday, September 27 (Moon into Pisces, 1:25 a.m.)   Finish what you've started. Clear your desk, and make way for the new. Look beyond the immediate. Let go of preconceived notions. Nurture your intuition. You can tap deeply into the collective unconscious for inspiration.

Friday, September 28 (Moon in Pisces)   The moon is in your ninth house today. That means it's a good time to start thinking about a long trip. Make your plans now. You're feeling restless. It's also a good time to explore ideas, philosophies, mythology. You're a dreamer and thinker now.

Saturday, September 29 (Moon into Aries, 9:15 a.m.)
There's a full moon in your tenth house today. That means you reap what you've sown related to your career. If you've performed well, it's time for a raise or advancement. You get a boost in your prestige. You gain insight and illumination about your profession.

Sunday, September 30 (Moon in Aries)   It's a great time for brainstorming new ideas. You're passionate but impatient. You're extremely persuasive now, especially if you're passionate about what you're doing, selling, or trying to convey. Have an adventure today; do something thrilling.

OCTOBER 2012

Monday, October 1 (Moon into Taurus, 7:27 p.m.)
Cooperation and partnerships are highlighted. You're diplomatic and capable of fixing whatever has gone wrong. As usual, you're concerned about keeping everything in balance, Cancer. That's your native energy. You excel in working with a group now. You're playing the role of the visionary today. Be honest and open.

Tuesday, October 2 (Moon in Taurus)   The moon is in your eleventh house today. Group activities are highlighted. You find strength in numbers now and meaning through friends and groups. Focus on your wishes and dreams. Your goals are achieved through help from friends and associates.

Wednesday, October 3 (Moon in Taurus)   Venus moves into your third house today. It's a good day for romance, possibly involving someone right in your neighborhood. You could be driving about town talking to the person. You've got lots of ideas about romance now, and much of it is related to your past.

Thursday, October 4 (Moon into Gemini, 7:47 a.m.) Do something different today. Take the day off; set off on a journey. Think freedom, no restrictions. Find a new point of view that fits current circumstances and what you know now. Let go of old structures. It's a good day to take a risk, experiment. Promote new ideas.

Friday, October 5 (Moon in Gemini) Mercury moves into your fifth house today. Your writing and speaking abilities are highlighted over the next two weeks. It's a good time for launching or working on a creative project. Meanwhile, Saturn also moves into your fifth house, where it will stay for two and a half years. That means you have better structure for creative venues. There could be some delays, especially if you try to take shortcuts. If you're looking for a new romance, you could get involved with someone older than you.

Saturday, October 6 (Moon into Cancer, 8:46 p.m.) With Mars moving into your sixth house, you're working hard this month with a new aggressiveness. You're annoyed by others who don't accommodate you or keep up with your pace. Be aware that if you push too hard, you could aggravate others and cause problems with your coworkers. Best advice for this month: control your temper.

Sunday, October 7 (Moon in Cancer)   The moon
is in your first house today. You're sensitive to other
people's feelings, especially family members and anyone else in your home. You feel moody one moment,
happy the next, then withdrawn and sad. It's all about
your emotional self. Your feelings and thoughts are
aligned. You're dealing with your emotional self, the
person you are becoming.

Monday, October 8 (Moon in Cancer)   With the
moon on your ascendant, your personality shines. You're
out in front of the public. Your face is all over Facebook.
You're recharged for the rest of the month, and this
makes you more appealing to the public. You're physically vital, and relations with the opposite sex go well.

Tuesday, October 9 (Moon into Leo, 7:55 a.m.)
It's a number 1 day, so you're at the top of your cycle
again. Get out and meet new people. In romance,
something new could be developing. A flirtation turns
more serious. You're inventive and make connections
that others overlook. You attract creative people now.

Wednesday, October 10 (Moon in Leo)   You feel
best sticking close to home today and surrounding
yourself with your favorite things. It's not the objects
that are important as the memories and feelings you
have related to them. Your values or ideals are important to you. Watch your spending, and look at your
priorities in handling your income.

Thursday, October 11 (Moon into Virgo, 3:24 p.m.)
You're innovative and creative and get your ideas

across. You could be expressing your ideas in e-mail, on blogs, or sending text messages to friends. Your popularity is on the rise, especially if you keep a positive attitude. You're warm and receptive to what others say. In romance, you're passionate and loyal.

Friday, October 12 (Moon in Virgo)   You let others know what you think about matters that are important to you. You especially express yourself to family members, relatives, and neighbors. Issues from the past could resurface, or you take an interest in important events from long ago that are shaping you and your world today.

Saturday, October 13 (Moon into Libra, 7:02 p.m.) Do something different today. Break the pattern. Promote new ideas; follow your curiosity. Look for adventure. Variety is the spice of life. You're seeking new horizons and ready to step out of the box.

Sunday, October 14 (Moon in Libra)   It's a good day to sleep late and remember your dreams. Write them down as soon as you get up. Pay attention to the symbols; look for meaning. Spend time at home with your family. As you know, there's nothing more important than that, Cancer. You feel a close tie to your roots.

Monday, October 15 (Moon into Scorpio, 8:07 p.m.) With the new moon in your fourth house, opportunities come your way related to your home. Your creativity flows best while you're in familiar surroundings, close to those you love. Someone might take an interest in your home and might even make an offer to buy it.

Tuesday, October 16 (Moon in Scorpio)   Love and creativity are highlighted today. Sex for pleasure might be on your agenda. There's greater emotional depth now in a relationship. It's a good day to take a chance, experiment, especially with a creative or artistic project. Children could play a significant role in your day.

Wednesday, October 17 (Moon into Sagittarius, 8:26 p.m.)   Finish whatever you've been working on and get ready for something new. Look for a new approach, a new perspective. You'll probably find that old ways have outlived their usefulness. Strive for universal appeal in whatever you're doing.

Thursday, October 18 (Moon in Sagittarius)   It's a good day to take care of any health or work issues. Keep your resolutions about exercise, and watch your diet. Take a yoga class. It's best if you follow a regular schedule now. Help others, but don't deny your own needs.

Friday, October 19 (Moon into Capricorn, 9:42 p.m.)   Use your intuition to get a sense of your day. Partnerships play an important role. Be kind and understanding. Don't make waves today; let things develop. Focus on your direction and motivation. Where are you going and why? Cooperation is highlighted.

Saturday, October 20 (Moon in Capricorn)   Your ambition and drive to succeed are highlighted. Your responsibilities increase. You might feel stressed, overworked, especially if your duties or studies extend into the weekend. Self-discipline and structure are key. Don't ignore your exercise routine. Banks and financial institutions could play a role in your day.

Sunday, October 21 (Moon in Capricorn)   With the moon in your seventh house, the focus turns to partnerships, both personal and business. A legal matter could be involved. Women play a prominent role. You get along well with others now, but don't let them manipulate your feelings.

Monday, October 22 (Moon into Aquarius, 1:03 a.m.)   Release old structures; get a new point of view. Change your perspective. (Easier said than done!) Think freedom, no restrictions. You can do that! Variety is the spice of life.

Tuesday, October 23 (Moon in Aquarius)   You could exploring mystical matters today. Woo-woo stuff. Friends play a role. Maybe you're talking about ghosts or visiting a haunted house. Something mysterious and out of the ordinary is in the air for you and certain friends.

Wednesday, October 24 (Moon into Pisces, 7:01 a.m.)   Yesterday's mysterious energy flows into your Wednesday. You launch a journey into the unknown. You investigate, analyze, or simply observe what's going on. You quickly come to a conclusion and wonder why others don't see what you see. Gather information, but don't make any absolute decisions until tomorrow.

Thursday, October 25 (Moon in Pisces)   You're a dreamer and a thinker, Cancer. Your imagination is highlighted. You're feeling restless and yearning for a new experience. Universal knowledge, eternal truths, deep spirituality are the themes of the day. Keep track of your dreams, including your daydreams. Ideas are ripe.

Friday, October 26 (Moon into Aries, 3:32 p.m.) Complete a project now. Clear up odds and ends. Clean a closet or your desk; put things away. Make room for something new. Accept what comes your way now, but don't start anything new until tomorrow.

Saturday, October 27 (Moon in Aries)   It's a great day for launching new ideas. You're extremely persuasive now, especially if you're passionate about what you're doing, selling, or trying to convey. You could be attending a sporting event today. Avoid reckless behavior. You're passionate but impatient.

Sunday, October 28 (Moon in Aries)   With Venus moving into your fourth house today, Cancer, your domestic life blossoms. Stick close to home; enjoy the love and affection. You feel a close tie to your roots, especially family members. A parent plays a role.

Monday, October 29 (Moon into Taurus, 2:16 a.m.) Mercury moves into Sagittarius, your sixth house, today, and that means there could be a lot of discussions in the workplace about expanding your role. There could be travel involved. You see the big picture now. There's also a full moon in your eleventh house, and that indicates that friends and associates help you achieve your wishes and dreams.

Tuesday, October 30 (Moon in Taurus)   The moon is in your eleventh house today. You work well with friends, especially on a project intended for the common good. Cultivate new ideas, but make sure that they're down-to-earth. Focus on your wishes and dreams, but use common sense in whatever you're doing.

Wednesday, October 31 (Moon into Gemini, 2:41 p.m.)   Get out today and explore. You're seeking new horizons. Travel and variety are highlighted. Approach the day with an unconventional mind-set. Take risks; experiment. A change of scenery would work to your advantage. You could be moving to a new location.

NOVEMBER 2012

Thursday, November 1 (Moon in Gemini)   Something from your past or childhood is on your mind. Unconscious attitudes can be difficult now. You communicate your deepest feelings to another person, but otherwise you keep your feelings secret. Your intuition is heightened. It's a great day for a mystical or spiritual discipline.

Friday, November 2 (Moon in Gemini)   Pay attention to any intuitive nudges you receive, especially related to your relationship with a woman. You're feeling restless today and sending text messages to friends and associates to pass the time. Your mind moves quickly from one thought to another. It's a good day to get together with old friends and talk over matters from the past.

Saturday, November 3 (Moon into Cancer, 3:43 a.m.) You're motivated and inspired. Travel and adventure are on the agenda. You're seeking new horizons, meeting new people now. Freedom of thought and action is key. You're courageous and adaptable.

Sunday, November 4—Daylight Saving Time Ends (Moon in Cancer) You're feeling on top of your game, and relations with the opposite sex go well. You shine before the public today. Your appearance and personality attract attention. You're recharged for the month.

Monday, November 5 (Moon into Leo, 3:40 p.m.) It's another mystery day as you look behind closed doors for answers. You're searching for the truth. You detect deception and recognize insincerity with ease. Express your desires, but avoid self-deception. Go with the flow.

Tuesday, November 6 (Moon in Leo) Mercury goes retrograde today in your sixth house and stays retrograde until November 26. That means you can expect some difficulties in your communication with a coworker or someone you're trying to help. You could be feeling uncertain or insecure about your ability to communicate effectively. A health issue could cause some confusion and misunderstanding.

Wednesday, November 7 (Moon in Leo) You could be feeling either upset and angry or joyous and thrilled about a money matter. You equate your financial assets with emotional security now. Look at your priorities in handling your income. You feel emotional about whatever you value or about the values you hold.

Thursday, November 8 (Moon into Virgo, 12:36 a.m.) It's a number 1 day, so you're at the top of your cycle. Your intuition is highlighted. You're inventive and make connections others overlook. You're determined and courageous today. Stress originality. Get out and meet new people. Express your opinions dynamically.

Friday, November 9 (Moon in Virgo) The moon is in your third house today. Your mental abilities are strong, and you have an emotional need to reinvigorate your studies. You could be exploring matters from the deep past. Share your knowledge with others. A short trip works to your benefit now.

Saturday, November 10 (Moon into Libra, 5:36 a.m.) Neptune goes direct in your ninth house today, where it stays for fourteen years. It forms a strong angle to the sun, so your ideas and ideals can be implemented on a broader scale over the coming months and years. You might be traveling overseas on a spiritual quest. If you're writing a novel, you could get it published. If you're involved in a green industry, it could expand overseas.

Sunday, November 11 (Moon in Libra)   The moon is in your fourth house, your native home, Cancer. That means your home life' is important now. Spend time with your family and loved ones. Stick close to home. You're dealing with the foundations of who you are and who you are becoming.

Monday, November 12 (Moon into Scorpio, 7:11 a.m.)   You're more comfortable than usual in front of an audience, especially if you approach the day with an unconventional mind-set. You're versatile and changeable. Get a new point of view. Promote new ideas; follow your curiosity.

Tuesday, November 13 (Moon in Scorpio)   There's a solar eclipse in your fifth house today. That's like a double new moon and means opportunities, especially related to a creative project. It could also mean the beginning of something new, such as a romance, or the end of one. Children could play an important role in your day.

Wednesday, November 14 (Moon into Sagittarius, 6:53 a.m.)   Mercury moves back to your fifth house today as it continues its retrograde motion. Computer glitches over the next two weeks could affect matters related to a creative project. There also could be confusion and miscommunication with a romantic partner. You can expect delays linked to activities with children. Leave plenty of time for short-distance travel.

Thursday, November 15 (Moon in Sagittarius)
The moon is in your sixth house today. You communicate your feelings well to coworkers, who are sympathetic, especially if you're dealing with plans to expand. Your life is more public now, so avoid emotional displays. You get along well with others in the workplace.

Friday, November 16 (Moon into Capricorn, 6:36 a.m.) Mars moves into your seventh house today. Your dealings with partners over the next three weeks could get intense. You're impulsive and aggressively push your point of view. Be aware that your actions could create some friction between you and your partner, whether it's a personal or business relationship.

Saturday, November 17 (Moon in Capricorn) The moon is in your seventh house today. Yesterday's energy flows into your Saturday. A legal matter comes to your attention now. Women play a prominent role. Be careful that others don't manipulate your feelings. You feel a need to be accepted. You're looking for security, but you have a hard time going with the flow.

Sunday, November 18 (Moon into Aquarius, 8:11 a.m.) It's a number 2 day, and that means cooperation is highlighted. Don't make waves. Don't rush or show resentment; let things develop. You're diplomatic and capable of fixing whatever has gone wrong.

Monday, November 19 (Moon in Aquarius) The moon is in your eighth house today. You're focusing on security issues now. You also have a strong sense of duty to helping others. You're sensitive to whatever is going on in the world that's attracting mass awareness. Take a look at your wishes and dreams. You get a new perspective.

Tuesday, November 20 (Moon into Pisces, 12:55 p.m.)   Persevere to get things done today. Don't get sloppy. Tear down the old in order to rebuild. Be methodical and thorough. Revise, rewrite. Clear your desk, or straighten up your garage or a closet.

Wednesday, November 21 (Moon in Pisces)   With Venus moving into Scorpio—your fifth house—for the next three weeks, your popularity is on the rise, and you're more appealing to the opposite sex. You're both passionate and loving, and you have a strong affection for children.

Thursday, November 22 (Moon into Aries, 9:12 p.m.)   Service to others is the theme of the day. Adjust to the needs of loved ones, and be diplomatic. A change in the home, an adjustment or readjustment, could be needed now. Don't put off the situation. That will only aggravate the problem.

Friday, November 23 (Moon in Aries)   The moon is in your tenth house today. It's a good day for sales and dealing with the public. You gain an elevation in prestige related to your career. Business dealings are highlighted. You're warmer and friendly toward coworkers, but don't make any emotional displays in public.

Saturday, November 24 (Moon in Aries)   You're extremely persuasive now, especially if you're passionate about what you're doing, selling, or trying to convey. Emotions could be volatile today. It's a great time for brainstorming or initiating new projects.

Sunday, November 25 (Moon into Taurus, 8:18 a.m.) Finish what you've started. Visualize the future; set your goals, then make them so. Clear up odds and ends. Take an inventory on where things are going in your life. It's a good day to make a donation to a worthy cause.

Monday, November 26 (Moon in Taurus)   Mercury goes direct in your fifth house today. Any confusion, miscommunication, and delays related to a romantic interest or a creative endeavor start to recede into the past. Things move more smoothly now. You get your message across, and everything works better, including computers and other electronic equipment.

Tuesday, November 27 (Moon into Gemini, 8:59 p.m.)   Your emotions and sensitivity are on high alert today. There could be some soul-searching related to relationships; or a new relationship could be forming. Help comes through friends or loved ones, especially a partner.

Wednesday, November 28 (Moon in Gemini) There's a lunar eclipse in your twelfth house today. That means something hidden surfaces, through news or an insight. The news should be good, and you should be able to use this information in a positive way. You could decide to build a blog or Web site.

Thursday, November 29 (Moon in Gemini) You tend to look inward now, and by doing so subconscious motivations surface and point you toward new ways to get your ideas across. It's a good day to withdraw from the action and work behind the scenes. You could be feeling especially sensitive. Matters from the past surface. Take time to relax and meditate.

Friday, November 30 (Moon into Cancer, 9:56 a.m.) Approach the day with an unconventional mind-set. Release old structures, and find a new point of view. Freedom of thought and action is key. But so is moderation; avoid excess in whatever you're doing. Get out and do something different. Variety is the spice of life.

DECEMBER 2012

Saturday, December 1 (Moon in Cancer) With the moon on your ascendant, you're recharged for the month ahead, and you're more appealing to the public. You're physically vital, and relations with the opposite sex go well. Your appearance and personality shine. Your feelings and thoughts are synchronized.

Sunday, December 2 (Moon into Leo, 9:58 p.m.) Think freedom, no restrictions today. A change of scenery would work to your advantage. Travel and variety are the order of the day or at least on your wish list. Look for something adventurous to do. Follow your curiosity. You're focused on the person you are becoming.

Monday, December 3 (Moon in Leo) It's a good day for finances. If you're involved in the stock market, you can cash in now. Your values are important and affect your decisions. Pay your bills, and collect what's owed to you. You identify emotionally with your possessions, which make you feel at home, Cancer.

Tuesday, December 4 (Moon in Leo) You're creative, passionate, and hungry for success today. You're also somewhat impulsive. Dress boldly now; showmanship is emphasized. You're at center stage. As yesterday, financial speculation plays a role. Oddly enough, so do animals and pets.

Wednesday, December 5 (Moon into Virgo, 7:53 a.m.) It's a number 8 day, your power day and your day to swing things your way. Unexpected money flows to you. Think big, and expect something big. Appear successful, even if you don't feel that way. You can go far with your plans and achieve financial success.

Thursday, December 6 (Moon in Virgo) Take what you know and tell others about it. Siblings, family, and neighbors play a role. Get your ideas and thoughts across, but keep conscious control of your emotions. Your thinking is unduly influenced by matters from the past. A short trip works to your benefit now.

Friday, December 7 (Moon into Libra, 2:37 p.m.)
You're at the top of your cycle again, Cancer. That means you can get a fresh start, or you can restart a delayed project. You also can take the lead. Don't be afraid to turn in a new direction. Your intuition is highlighted. In romance, something new could be developing, if that's what you want.

Saturday, December 8 (Moon in Libra) The moon is in your fourth house today, your native home, Cancer. It's a perfect day for spending time with your family and loved ones. Stick close to home. Work on a home-repair project, something to beautify your environment. You feel a close tie to your roots. A parent could play an important role in your day.

Sunday, December 9 (Moon into Scorpio, 5:52 p.m.)
You're innovative and creative and communicate well now. Your charm and wit are appreciated. Your attitude determines everything today. Remain flexible and open to sudden opportunity. In romance, you're an ardent and loyal lover.

Monday, December 10 (Moon in Scorpio) Mercury moves into your sixth house today. That means that your communication with coworkers improves. You help others solve problems and mediate disagreements. You explain clearly all that needs to be said. You're very methodical and efficient in handling your duties, especially those of a mental nature. You also could be talking more with others about a health issue.

Tuesday, December 11 (Moon into Sagittarius, 6:22 p.m.) Variety is the spice of life. Help others, but think outside the box. Take risks; experiment. Let go of old structures. Get a new point of view, especially related to the workplace. You're versatile and changeable, but be careful not to spread out and diversify too much.

Wednesday, December 12 (Moon in Sagittarius) It's another service day. You're the one others go to for assistance. You improve, refine, and edit their work. Attend to daily details, and be of service. Help your coworkers, but don't overlook your own needs. Make appointments that you've been putting off.

Thursday, December 13 (Moon into Capricorn, 5:43 p.m.) Uranus goes direct in your tenth house today. You take an offbeat approach to your career over coming months and years. You could lose your job and find a better one. Think outside the box in your professional life now. Go with the flow. Also, with a new moon today in your sixth house, you should find new opportunities immediately in your workplace, especially if you're working to help others.

Friday, December 14 (Moon in Capricorn) Personal relationships take on greater meaning today. You feel a need to be accepted. You can fit in just about anywhere. Be careful that others don't manipulate your feelings. Women play a prominent role.

Saturday, December 15 (Moon into Aquarius, 5:53 p.m.) With Venus moving into your sixth house for the next three weeks, you could be feeling emotionally attached to your work or your workplace this month. Romance in the workplace is a possibility now. You also could act as a mediator, settling a dispute among fellow workers.

Sunday, December 16 (Moon in Aquarius)   You could find yourself in a disagreement with a spouse or partner related to finances—a mortgage, insurance, or an inheritance. Focus on your wishes and dreams, but make sure that you and your partner are in agreement. Otherwise, you could encounter intense emotional resistance.

Monday, December 17 (Moon into Pisces, 8:48 p.m.) As yesterday, partnerships are highlighted. Your intuition focuses on relationships. You excel in working with others now. You're playing the role of the visionary today. You're concerned about your home, your security, or a parent, Cancer. Avoid becoming caught up in the collective muck related to fears of the upcoming end of the Mayan Calendar on December 21.

Tuesday, December 18 (Moon in Pisces)   The moon is in your ninth house today. You're in touch with your creative side. You have a strong curiosity now about foreign cultures. It's a great time to improve your skills with a foreign language. Long-distance travel is on your mind, especially related to your higher mind or higher education.

Wednesday, December 19 (Moon in Pisces)   Keep track of your dreams, including your daydreams. Ideas are ripe now. It's a day for deep healing. Universal knowledge, eternal truths, deep spirituality are other themes of the day.

Thursday, December 20 (Moon into Aries, 3:44 a.m.)
It's a number 5 day, and that means it's a good time to promote new ideas. You're versatile, changeable. Be careful not to spread out and diversify too much. Freedom of thought and action is key. A change of scenery would work to your advantage. Avoid becoming caught up in the collective fears related to the end of the world.

Friday, December 21 (Moon in Aries) The Mayan Calendar ends today! The old world ends; the new one begins. Look for transformation on a large scale as the old paradigm fades. With the moon in your tenth house, you communicate your feelings clearly to coworkers, who are sympathetic, and you get along well with them. Your life is more public now, so avoid emotional displays. Be careful about mixing your personal and professional lives.

Saturday, December 22 (Moon into Taurus, 2:26 p.m.) It's a mystery day, time to explore the unknown. Look behind closed doors. Dig deep for information now, but don't make any absolute decisions until tomorrow. Express your desires, but avoid self-deception. You work best on your own today.

Sunday, December 23 (Moon in Taurus) Friends play a key role in helping you fulfill your wishes and dreams. You get along well with groups, especially when everyone is of like mind with a down-to-earth perspective. You help the group's goals, and you benefit in return.

Monday, December 24 (Moon in Taurus)   Health and physical activity are highlighted. It's a good day to use common sense and take a practical approach to whatever you're doing, Cancer. Take care of money issues now. Try to avoid stubborn behavior when others question your actions.

Tuesday, December 25 (Moon into Gemini, 3:14 a.m.)   Mars moves into your eighth house today. You investigate a matter of some importance that could involve finances, insurance, a mortgage, or an inheritance. You tend to act aggressively regarding any joint ventures or shared resources. Thanks to Mars, your sexual drive is also enhanced. Merry Christmas!

Wednesday, December 26 (Moon in Gemini)   The moon is in your twelfth house today. You could be feeling confused about the direction of your life. You might feel a need to withdraw and work on your own. Think carefully before you act. There's a tendency now to undo all the positive actions you've taken. Avoid any self-destructive tendencies. Be aware of hidden enemies.

Thursday, December 27 (Moon into Cancer, 4:08 p.m.)   Others see you as optimistic now. Your charm and wit are appreciated. Spread your good news, and take time to listen to others. Remain flexible, open to change. Follow your intuition. Relax and enjoy yourself.

Friday, December 28 (Moon in Cancer)   There's a full moon in your sign today, Cancer. New opportunities present themselves related to personal growth. Maybe you want to sell your house and move or embark on a new romance. Whatever your personal desires are, you have the chance now to fulfill those dreams.

Saturday, December 29 (Moon in Cancer)   You're recharged for the month ahead, and this makes you more appealing to everyone you encounter. Your feelings and thoughts are aligned today. Your self-awareness and appearance are particularly important now. You're dealing with the person you want to become.

Sunday, December 30 (Moon into Leo, 3:47 a.m.) Diplomacy wins the day. A change in the home, an adjustment or readjustment, is needed now. Don't put off the situation. That will only aggravate the problem. Be sympathetic and compassionate, but avoid scattering your energies. Focus on making people happy.

Monday, December 31 (Moon in Leo)   Mercury moves into your seventh house today. You've got lots of ideas, and you're forthright in offering them. You and a partner communicate well. You're good at promoting your ideas and marketing yourself. You get along well with others now. You can fit in just about anywhere.

HAPPY NEW YEAR!

Tuesday, January 1 (Moon into Virgo, 12:36 p.m.)
You're innovative and creative and communicate well today, Cancer. Your attitude determines everything. Spread your good news, and take time to listen to others. You're warm and receptive to what they say. Your charm and wit are appreciated.

Wednesday, January 2 (Moon in Virgo) The moon is in your third house today. Your mental abilities are strong now, and you have an emotional need to reinvigorate your studies, especially regarding matters of the past. As you go about your everyday life, look to the past for clues about what's coming up in the near future. You also could be exploring matters from the deep past, including historical or archaeological documents.

Thursday, January 3 (Moon into Libra, 8:12 p.m.)
Variety is the spice of life today, Cancer. You're seeking new horizons. Think outside the box. Take risks; experiment. Release old structures; get a new point of view. Freedom of thought and action is key. But so is moderation; avoid excess in whatever you're doing.

Friday, January 4 (Moon in Libra) The moon is in your fourth house today. Get organized now. You're dealing with foundations, the very foundations of who you are and who you are becoming. Make an effort to change a bad habit. It's best to work on your own. Stay focused, and don't let others distract you.

Saturday, January 5 (Moon in Libra) Relationship issues figure prominently in your day. Romance is highlighted. Museums, art, music, creativity all figure in. It's a day for feeding your creative juices. Your personal grace, magnetism, physical attraction play a role.

Sunday, January 6 (Moon into Scorpio, 1:10 a.m.) It's a number 8 day, your power day and your day to play it your way. Unexpected money arrives. You can go far with your plans and achieve financial success. Be aware that you're playing with power, so try not to hurt anyone. Act with courage and honesty.

Monday, January 7 (Moon in Scorpio) The moon is in your fifth house today. It's a great day for pursuing a romance. There's greater emotional depth in whatever you pursue. Be yourself; be emotionally honest. You're creative now and have the ability to tap deeply into the collective unconscious. Children and pets could play a role.

Tuesday, January 8 (Moon into Sagittarius, 3:29 a.m.) It's a number 1 day, and you're at the top of your cycle, Cancer. You can take the lead today. You get a fresh start, a new beginning. Don't be afraid to turn in a new direction. Stress originality, and refuse to deal with people who have closed minds.

Wednesday, January 9 (Moon in Sagittarius) Venus moves into your seventh house today. You're starting the year on a high note. You find harmony in a professional or personal relationship now. You get along well with others. You could gain financially through a marriage or partnership.

Thursday, January 10 (Moon into Capricorn, 3:55 a.m.)   It's a number 4 day. That means the emphasis today is on your organizational skills. In romance your persistence pays off. You're building a foundation for the future. Control your impulses to wander; fulfill your obligations. You could find missing papers now.

Friday, January 11 (Moon in Capricorn)   There's a new moon in your seventh house today. That means new opportunities come your way. Partnerships are explored in a new venture or adventure. Don't let your fears hold you back. Loved ones and partners are more important than usual.

Saturday, January 12 (Moon into Aquarius, 4:02 a.m.)   Domestic purchases are highlighted. Focus on making people happy. Do a good deed. It's a service day, so direct your energy toward helping others, Cancer. Be generous and tolerant, even if it goes against your nature.

Sunday, January 13 (Moon in Aquarius)   The moon is in your eighth house today. You could be attracting powerful people to you. Your experiences could be intense, especially related to shared belongings. An interest in metaphysics plays a role.

Monday, January 14 (Moon into Pisces, 5:50 a.m.) It's a number 8 day, your power day. Expect a financial windfall. It's a good day to play the lotto. Business dealings go well, and a new approach brings in big bucks.

Tuesday, January 15 (Moon in Pisces)   With the moon in your ninth house now, it's a good time to look to the big picture. Break away from your routine or the usual way you think about things. You could be feeling restless and looking for a broader approach, for new information, new ideas. A foreign-born person or a foreign country could play a role.

Wednesday, January 16 (Moon into Aries, 11:08 a.m.)   You're at the top of your cycle again. Be independent and creative, and refuse to be discouraged by naysayers. Trust your hunches; your intuition is highlighted. Get out and meet new people. You attract creative people to your cause.

Thursday, January 17 (Moon in Aries)   The moon is in your tenth house today. Professional concerns are the focus of the day. You gain an elevation in prestige or a promotion. You get along well with fellow workers, who are appreciative. You're in the public eye now, so it's best to avoid any emotional displays.

Friday, January 18 (Moon into Taurus, 8:37 p.m.) You communicate well today. Enjoy the harmony, beauty, and pleasures of life. Beautify your home. Remain flexible. Your imagination is keen now. You're curious and inventive. You're warm and receptive to what others say.

Saturday, January 19 (Moon in Taurus)   Mercury moves into your eighth house today, the house of shared resources. It's a good day for dealing with mortgages, insurance, and investments. You could be managing and controlling the resources of others. Meanwhile, mysteries of the unknown attract your attention, distracting you from more mundane activities.

Sunday, January 20 (Moon in Taurus)   With the moon in your eleventh house, friends play an important role in your day and help you in surprising ways. You work well with a group of like-minded people. Focus on your wishes and dreams, and make sure that they are an expression of who you really are.

Monday, January 21 (Moon into Gemini, 9:06 a.m.) It's a number 6 day. Be understanding, and avoid confrontations. Diplomacy wins the way. Focus on making people happy, but avoid scattering your energies. Be sympathetic, kind, and compassionate. A domestic shift of priorities might be needed now, Cancer.

Tuesday, January 22 (Moon in Gemini)   The moon is in your twelfth house today. Think carefully before you act. There's a tendency now to undo all the positive actions you've taken. Avoid any self-destructive behavior. It's best to work behind the scenes and stay out of the public view. Be aware of hidden enemies.

Wednesday, January 23 (Moon into Cancer, 10:01 p.m.)   It's your mystery day, Cancer. You journey into the unknown, digging deep for information. Secrets, intrigue, confidential information play a role. Be aware of decisions made behind closed doors. Go with the flow. Express your desires, but avoid self-deception.

Thursday, January 24 (Moon in Cancer) With the moon on your ascendant, you're feeling recharged. You face is in the public. Maybe your face is all over Facebook today. You're physically vital, and relations with the opposite sex go well. Your appearance and personality shine.

Friday, January 25 (Moon in Cancer) You're somewhat moody today, Cancer, and sensitive to other people's feelings. You feel happy one moment, withdrawn and sad the next. It's all about your health and your emotional self: how you feel and how you feel about yourself. Your feelings and thoughts are aligned.

Saturday, January 26 (Moon into Leo, 9:21 a.m.) With the full moon in your second house, it's a good money day. You reap what you've sown. Look at your priorities in handling your income. You've got a better understanding now of your financial status. You get a new perspective.

Sunday, January 27 (Moon in Leo) Yesterday's energy flows into your Sunday. You feel best now surrounded by familiar objects, your stuff. It's not the objects themselves that are important, but the feelings and memories you associate with them. Put off making any major purchases. You equate your financial assets with emotional security.

Monday, January 28 (Moon into Virgo, 6:28 p.m.)
It's a number 3 day. Have fun today in preparation for tomorrow's discipline and focus. Make time to listen to others. Your charm and wit are appreciated. Spread your good news; you communicate well.

Tuesday, January 29 (Moon in Virgo)   The moon is in your third house today. A short trip works to your benefit now. You write from a deep place; it's a good day for journaling. Your thinking may be unduly influenced by things from the past. Female relatives play a role.

Wednesday, January 30 (Moon in Virgo)   Jupiter goes direct in your twelfth house today. That means you have an opportunity to expand whatever you're doing. It's best to keep your thoughts to yourself and work behind the scenes. Be aware of hidden enemies, who might target your bold plans. You're looking at the big picture related to your past. Take time to reflect and meditate.

Thursday, January 31 (Moon into Libra, 1:36 a.m.)
It's a number 6 day, a service-oriented day. You offer advice and support to those around you. Do a good deed for someone. Be sympathetic and kind, generous and tolerant. Diplomacy wins the way. An adjustment in your domestic life may be necessary now.

FEBRUARY 2013

Friday, February 1 (Moon in Libra)   With Venus moving into your eighth house today, there could be

234

financial gain through a partnership or marriage this month. There might be an inheritance involved, or you could get a break on mortgage, loans, insurance, or taxes. Meanwhile, with Mars moving into your ninth house, you aggressively pursue an interest in higher education or long-distance travel.

Saturday, February 2 (Moon into Scorpio, 7:02 a.m.) It's a number 5 day. That means change and variety are highlighted now. Think freedom; think outside the box. No restrictions. Your creativity, personal grace, and magnetism are highlighted.

Sunday, February 3 (Moon in Scorpio) The moon is in your fifth house today, and that means romance is in the air, Cancer. Communication with a loved one is strengthened by emotion, which can take you one step closer to commitment. But try not to be overly possessive. It's also a good day for pursuing a creative project. You get a breakthrough. Children could be involved.

Monday, February 4 (Moon into Sagittarius, 10:46 a.m.) It's a number 7 day, your mystery day, Cancer. You venture into the unknown now. You investigate, analyze, or just quietly observe what's going on. Knowledge is essential to success. Gather information, but don't make any absolute decisions until tomorrow.

Tuesday, February 5 (Moon in Sagittarius) With Mercury moving into your ninth house today, it's a great time to pursue plans for higher education or taking a long trip. You write and speak well on matters related to your philosophy of life. You make your point and are understood.

Wednesday, February 6 (Moon into Capricorn, 12:56 p.m.)   It's a number 9 day. Use the day for reflection, expansion, and concluding projects. Clear up odds and ends. Take an inventory on where things are going in your life. Make room for something new. Visualize the future; set your goals, then make them so.

Thursday, February 7 (Moon in Capricorn)   The moon is in your seventh house today as the focus turns to partnerships, both personal and business. A legal matter could be involved. Women play a prominent role. You get along well with others now, but be careful that they don't manipulate your feelings.

Friday, February 8 (Moon into Aquarius, 2:18 p.m.) It's a number 2 day. That means that cooperation and partnership are highlighted again. There's a new beginning now, or a new opportunity arises. Your intuition focuses on relationships. Don't make waves. Don't rush or show resentment; let things develop.

Saturday, February 9 (Moon in Aquarius)   The moon is in your eighth house today. Things could get emotionally intense in your dealings with someone of the opposite sex. That's particularly true if you're facing issues related to shared belongings. You're sensitive and intuitive now, and you could take an interest in a metaphysical topic, such as past lives.

Sunday, February 10 (Moon into Pisces, 4:21 p.m.)
There's a new moon in your eighth house today. That means there are opportunities related to a partnership that could result in more income. Any matters related to an inheritance, insurance, or taxes work to your advantage now. You also could take a closer look at a paranormal subject, possibly astrology.

Monday, February 11 (Moon in Pisces)   With the moon in your ninth house, you're feeling restless planning an escape from the routine, Cancer. Long-distance travel for pleasure is indicated. In romance a flirtation with a foreign-born person could turn serious. A love of philosophy and other intellectual interests could play a role.

Tuesday, February 12 (Moon into Aries, 8:53 p.m.)
Service to others is the theme of the day. Diplomacy wins the way. Focus on making people happy. You offer advice and support. Be sympathetic and kind, but avoid scattering your energies.

Wednesday, February 13 (Moon in Aries)   The moon is in your tenth house today, and that means professional concerns take priority. It's a good day for sales, dealing with the public. You're more responsive to the needs of others, especially coworkers. However, control your emotions in public, Cancer. Also, best to avoid mixing your personal and professional lives.

Thursday, February 14 (Moon in Aries)   It's a great time for initiating projects, launching new ideas, brainstorming. Emotions could be volatile. You're

237

passionate but impatient. You're extremely persuasive now, especially if you're passionate about what you're doing, selling, or trying to convey. Imprint your style.

Friday, February 15 (Moon into Taurus, 5:09 a.m.)
Use the day for reflection, expansion, and concluding projects. Take an inventory on where things are going in your life. Make room for something new, but don't start anything until next week.

Saturday, February 16 (Moon in Taurus) The moon is in your eleventh house today. While yesterday you were finishing something and getting ready for something new, today you spend time with friends, possibly in a group activity. You get along well with others. You work for the common good, and others support your wishes and dreams.

Sunday, February 17 (Moon into Gemini, 4:51 p.m.)
It's a number 2 day, and that means partnership is the theme of your day. Your spouse or partner is at your side. Don't make waves or show resentment, but take time to consider the direction you're headed and your motivation for continuing on this path. Your intuition focuses on relationships.

Monday, February 18 (Moon in Gemini) Saturn turns retrograde in your fifth house and stays that way until July 7. That means you could have a problem with a romance or with a child or children over the coming weeks and months, especially if you're denying your own needs. You also could feel some emotional constraints related to a creative project. You might need to refocus your energy and work behind the scenes. It's time to lay a better foundation for a relationship or a creative endeavor. It's a challenging time, but you can come out the better for it.

Tuesday, February 19 (Moon in Gemini) The moon is in your twelfth house today. Think carefully before you act. There's a tendency now to undo all the positive actions you've taken. Avoid any self-destructive behavior. It's best to work behind the scenes and stay out of the public view. Be aware of hidden enemies.

Wednesday, February 20 (Moon into Cancer, 5:45 a.m.) It's a number 5 day. Variety is the spice of life. Think freedom, no restrictions. Promote new ideas; follow your curiosity. Look for adventure. Think outside the box. You can overcome obstacles with ease.

Thursday, February 21 (Moon in Cancer) The moon is on your ascendant today. The way you see yourself now is the way others see you. Your face is before the public. You're recharged for the month ahead, and this makes you more appealing.

Friday, February 22 (Moon into Leo, 5:12 p.m.) It's a number 7 day. You investigate, analyze, or simply observe what's going on now. You quickly come to a conclusion and wonder why others don't see what you see. You detect deception and recognize insincerity with ease.

Saturday, February 23 (Moon in Leo) Mercury goes retrograde in your ninth house today. That means you can expect some delays and confusion in communication over the next three weeks. That's especially true if you're planning a long trip or dealing with higher education. When talking to anyone about your plans, be sure to make yourself clearly understood. There also could be some glitches with a computer or other electronic devices. It all ends on March 17.

Sunday, February 24 (Moon in Leo) The moon is in your second house today. Expect emotional experiences related to money. You identify emotionally with your possessions or whatever you value. Look at your priorities in handling your income. Put off making any major purchases now.

Monday, February 25 (Moon into Virgo, 1:53 a.m.) With Venus moving into your ninth house, your love of travel and study abroad is highlighted. Plan a long trip. You're a dreamer and a thinker. Your mind is active, and you yearn for new experiences, a break from the routine, a change from the status quo. With the full moon in your third house today, you reap what you have sown. You connect with siblings or other relatives, but control your emotions when talking with them.

Tuesday, February 26 (Moon in Virgo) With the moon in your third house today, some of yesterday's energy flows into your Tuesday. Your thinking is influenced by matters of the past, especially related to siblings and other relatives. You also could be exploring matters from the deep past. You communicate well, but control your emotions when you make your point.

Wednesday, February 27 (Moon into Libra, 8:02 a.m.)   You're innovative and creative and communicate well. Enjoy the harmony, beauty, and pleasures of life, Cancer. Beautify your home. Remain flexible. Your attitude determines everything today. Spread your good news. Ease up on routines.

Thursday, February 28 (Moon in Libra)   The moon is in your fourth house, your native home, Cancer. You feel very attached to your home life now. You get along well with family and other loved ones. You enjoy beautifying your home. You feel close to a parent or parents.

MARCH 2013

Friday, March 1 (Moon into Scorpio, 12:34 p.m.) It's a number 5 day. Variety is the spice of life. You're seeking new horizons. Think outside the box. Take risks; experiment. You can multitask efficiently today. Release old structures; get a new point of view.

Saturday, March 2 (Moon in Scorpio)   The moon is in your fifth house today. New opportunities appear now related to a creative project. It's a good day to take a chance. Be yourself; be emotionally honest. Be aware that your emotions tend to overpower your intellect.

Sunday, March 3 (Moon into Sagittarius, 4:11 p.m.)
You investigate, analyze, or simply observe what's going on now. You quickly come to a conclusion and wonder why others don't see what you see. You detect deception and recognize insincerity with ease.

Monday, March 4 (Moon in Sagittarius)   With the moon in your sixth house today, the emphasis turns to your daily work and service to others. Attend to all the details, Cancer. Be careful not to overlook any seemingly minor matters that could take on importance. Keep up with your exercise plan, and watch your diet.

Tuesday, March 5 (Moon into Capricorn, 7:15 p.m.)
Wrap up a project, and prepare for something new. Take time to reflect on everything that's been going on. Look for a way to expand your horizons, but don't start anything new until tomorrow.

Wednesday, March 6 (Moon in Capricorn)   With the moon in your seventh house today, Cancer, you turn your focus to partnerships, both business and personal. A legal matter could come to your attention now. You comprehend the nuances of a situation, but it's difficult to go with the flow. Be careful that others don't manipulate your feelings.

Thursday, March 7 (Moon into Aquarius, 10:03 p.m.)   It's all about cooperation and partnerships now. Concentrate more on your relationships. It's good to build those friendships and offer support where it is needed. You're diplomatic and capable of fixing whatever has gone wrong.

Friday, March 8 (Moon in Aquarius)   The moon is in your eighth house today. Your experiences are more intense than usual. Security is an important issue with you right now. It can affect your feelings about your belongings, as well as things that you share with others, such as a spouse. You have a strong sense of duty and feel obligated to fulfill your promises.

Saturday, March 9 (Moon in Aquarius)   Your individuality is stressed today, Cancer. Your visionary abilities are heightened. You have a greater sense of freedom now. You're dealing with new ideas, new options, originality. It's time to get a new perspective. Play your hunches. Look beyond the immediate.

Sunday, March 10—Daylight Saving Time Begins (Moon into Pisces, 1:20 a.m.)   Yesterday's energy flows into your Sunday. Change and variety are highlighted now. Think freedom, no restrictions. Release old structures; get a new point of view. It's a good day to take a risk, experiment. Promote new ideas. Find a new point of view that fits current circumstances and what you know now.

Monday, March 11 (Moon in Pisces)   There's a new moon in your ninth house today, and that indicates a new opportunity related to higher education or long-distance travel. You may feel a need to get away now, a break from the usual routine. You yearn for a new experience. Sign up for a workshop or seminar or plan a long trip. Alternately, you get a break on a publishing project.

Tuesday, March 12 (Moon into Aries, 6:18 a.m.)
Mars moves into your tenth house today. You're ready to make some aggressive professional moves over the next three weeks. You're seeking a promotion, a raise, an elevation in status and prestige. You take the initiative now. It's a good day for sales, dealing with the public. However, take care to avoid emotional displays, especially in public.

Wednesday, March 13 (Moon in Aries)   With the moon in your tenth house today, yesterday's energy flows strongly into your Wednesday. You're focused on your career. You could be looking for a more public position now. Friendly coworkers are on your side.

Thursday, March 14 (Moon into Taurus, 2:09 p.m.)
It's a number 9 day. Complete a project now. Clear up odds and ends. Take an inventory on where things are going in your life. Visualize the future; set your goals, then make them so. Accept what comes your way now. It's all part of a cycle.

Friday, March 15 (Moon in Taurus)   The moon is in your eleventh house today. Friends play an important role in your day, especially Scorpio and Pisces. You get together with a group of like-minded individuals and work toward a common goal. Focus on your wishes and dreams, and make sure that they are still a reflection of who you are.

Saturday, March 16 (Moon in Taurus) It's a good day to cultivate new ideas, but make sure that they're down to earth. You're feeling strong willed today, but avoid stubborn behavior. Health and physical activity are highlighted. Tend to money matters, and use your common sense.

Sunday, March 17 (Moon into Gemini, 1:10 a.m.) Mercury goes direct in your ninth house today. Any confusion, miscommunication, and delays start to recede into the past. Things move more smoothly now, especially related to long-distance travel or higher education. You get your message across, especially if a foreign-born person plays a role. Everything works better, including computers and other electronic equipment.

Monday, March 18 (Moon in Gemini) The moon is in your twelfth house today. It's a good day to work behind the scenes and avoid any conflict, especially with women. You could be dealing with a matter from the past that has returned to haunt you. Keep your feelings secret. Follow your intuition. Think freedom, no restrictions.

Tuesday, March 19 (Moon into Cancer, 1:56 p.m.) It's a good day to take a risk, experiment. Promote new ideas. Find a new point of view that fits current circumstances and what you know now. Change and variety are highlighted.

Wednesday, March 20 (Moon in Cancer) The moon is on your ascendant today. The way you see yourself now is the way others see you. You're recharged for the rest of the month, and this makes you more appealing to the public. You're physically vital, and relations with the opposite sex go well.

Thursday, March 21 (Moon in Cancer)   Venus moves into your tenth house today, indicating that it's a good time to promote your career goals. You should feel especially comfortable and happy in your career over the next three weeks. You get along well with others in the workplace. A flirtation with a colleague could turn into something more serious, if that's what you want.

Friday, March 22 (Moon into Leo, 1:50 a.m.)   It's a number 8 day, your power day. It's a good day to buy a lotto ticket. You pull off a financial coup. Business dealings go well. Expect a windfall. Appear successful now, even if you don't feel that way. Financial gain is at hand.

Saturday, March 23 (Moon in Leo)   The moon is in your second house today. Money and material goods are important to you now and give you a sense of security. You identify emotionally with your possessions or whatever you value. Put off making any major purchases. Look at your priorities in handling your income.

Sunday, March 24 (Moon into Virgo, 10:50 a.m.) It's a number 1 day, and you're at the top of your cycle again. You're inventive and make connections that others overlook. You're determined and courageous today. Explore, discover, create. Express your opinions dynamically. Get out and meet new people, have new experiences, do something you've never done before.

Monday, March 25 (Moon in Virgo)   The moon is in your third house today. A short trip works to your benefit now. Your mental abilities are strong, and you have an emotional need to reinvigorate your studies, especially regarding matters of the past. You're attracted to historical or archaeological studies.

Tuesday, March 26 (Moon into Libra, 4:33 p.m.) It's a number 3 day. Your attitude determines everything today, Cancer. You communicate well now. You're curious and inventive; ideas bubble forth. Your imagination is keen. Your popularity is on the rise.

Wednesday, March 27 (Moon in Libra)   There's a full moon in your fourth house today. You're emotionally in touch with your domestic life now, and you gain insight and illumination related to a creative project. It's a time of completion. You might be somewhat possessive of loved ones, particularly children.

Thursday, March 28 (Moon into Scorpio, 7:55 p.m.) Change and variety are highlighted now. Think freedom, no restrictions. Release old structures; get a new point of view. It's a good day to take a risk, experiment. Promote new ideas. Find a new outlook that feels right.

Friday, March 29 (Moon in Scorpio)   The moon is in your fifth house today. Be yourself; be emotionally honest. In love there's greater emotional depth to a relationship. You're emotionally in touch with your creative side now. You might be somewhat possessive of loved ones, particularly children.

Saturday, March 30 (Moon into Sagittarius, 10:14 p.m.)   Secrets, intrigue, confidential information play a role in your day. Dig deep and gather information, but don't make any absolute decisions until tomorrow. Go with the flow. Maintain your emotional balance. Avoid confusion and conflicts.

Sunday, March 31 (Moon in Sagittarius)   The moon is in your sixth house today. It's a service day. You're the one others go to for help. Offer assistance, but don't deny your own needs. It's best if you follow a regular schedule now. It's a good day to clarify any health or work issues.

APRIL 2013

Monday, April 1 (Moon in Sagittarius)   It's a service day. Adjust to the needs of loved ones. You offer advice and support. Be sympathetic and kind, generous and tolerant. A change in the home, an adjustment or readjustment, is needed now. Don't put off the situation. That will only aggravate the problem.

Tuesday, April 2 (Moon into Capricorn, 12:36 a.m.) It's a number 7 day, a mystery day. You launch a journey into the unknown. Secrets, intrigue, confidential information play a role. You work best on your own today. Knowledge is essential to success. Gather information, but don't make any absolute decisions until tomorrow.

Wednesday, April 3 (Moon in Capricorn)   The moon is in your seventh house today. The focus is on relationships, business and personal ones. You comprehend the nuances of a situation, but it's difficult to go with the flow. You feel a need to be accepted, but be careful that others don't manipulate your feelings.

Thursday, April 4 (Moon into Aquarius, 3:42 a.m.) It's a number 9 day. Finish what you started. Make room for something new. Clear your desk for tomorrow's new cycle, then look beyond the immediate. Strive for universal appeal.

Friday, April 5 (Moon in Aquarius)   The moon is in your eighth house today. You're attracted to psychic exploration, including contact with the other side. Your intuition is enhanced. Alternately, you could be involved in managing joint finances or shared possessions now.

Saturday, April 6 (Moon into Pisces, 8:01 a.m.) It's a number 2 day, putting the spotlight on cooperation. Help comes through friends or loved ones, especially a partner. Don't make waves. Don't rush or show resentment; let things develop. There could be some soul-searching related to a relationship now.

Sunday, April 7 (Moon in Pisces)   The moon is in your ninth house today. You're a dreamer and a thinker. You may feel a need to get away now, a break from the usual routine. Plan a long trip. Sign up for a workshop or seminar. Publicize and advertise whatever you're doing. If you're involved with a publishing project, expect some answers—positive ones.

Monday, April 8 (Moon into Aries, 2:03 p.m.) It's a number 4 day. That means your organizational skills are called upon, Cancer. Persevere to get things done today. Hard work is called for. Be methodical and thorough. Tear down the old in order to rebuild. You're developing a creative base for the future.

Tuesday, April 9 (Moon in Aries) The moon is in your tenth house today. You gain a big boost in prestige related to your profession. Business dealings go well. Your life is more public than usual. You're more emotional and warm toward coworkers, but be careful about mixing your personal and professional lives.

Wednesday, April 10 (Moon into Taurus, 10:22 p.m.) There's a new moon in your tenth house today and also six planets in Aries. It's all about opportunities that come your way related to your career. It's a great time to start something new that enhances your career. Whatever it is, the energy is strong and could dramatically change your life.

Thursday, April 11 (Moon in Taurus) The moon is in your eleventh house today. Friends play an important role in your day, especially Scorpio and Pisces. You work well with others, especially in a group, and you communicate well. Focus on your wishes and dreams. Examine your overall goals, and make sure that they're still an expression of who you are.

Friday, April 12 (Moon in Taurus)   Pluto goes retrograde in your seventh house today, Cancer, and stays that way until September 9. That means things get bogged down related to a partnership or contract. It takes longer to accomplish whatever you're trying to achieve, especially if there's another person or persons involved. You tend to look inward more often and consider whether or not you're following the career or personal path that's most appropriate for you.

Saturday, April 13 (Moon into Gemini, 9:13 a.m.) Mercury moves into your tenth house today, Cancer. Your speaking and writing abilities flourish now. You communicate well to the public, and you can bolster your career. You gain recognition for what you do.

Sunday, April 14 (Moon in Gemini)   The moon is in your twelfth house today. You might feel a need to withdraw and work on your own. Watch what you say, and think carefully before you act. There's a tendency now to undo all the positive actions you've taken. Avoid any self-destructive behavior. Be aware of hidden enemies.

Monday, April 15 (Moon into Cancer, 9:50 p.m.) Venus moves into your eleventh house today, where it stays until May 9. There's nothing better now than to spend time with friends or a group of like-minded people. You get along well with others and have deeper relationships with friends. Focus on your wishes and dreams, and know that they will come true.

Tuesday, April 16 (Moon in Cancer)   The moon is in your first house today. You're sensitive to other people's feelings now. You may feel moody one moment, happy the next, then withdrawn and sad. It's all about your health and your emotional self: how you feel and how you feel about yourself. It's difficult to remain detached and objective.

Wednesday, April 17 (Moon in Cancer)   The moon is on your ascendant. It's a great time to start something new. Your appearance and personality shine. Your feelings and thoughts are aligned today. The way you see yourself now is the way others see you. You're recharged for the month ahead, and this makes you more appealing to the public.

Thursday, April 18 (Moon into Leo, 10:15 a.m.) Change and variety are highlighted now. Think freedom, no restrictions. Find a new point of view that fits current circumstances and what you know. Release old structures; get a new point of view. It's a good day to take a risk, experiment. Promote new ideas.

Friday, April 19 (Moon in Leo)   The moon is in your second house today, Cancer. You feel strongly about a money issue. Finances and material goods are important to you now and give you a sense of security. You identify emotionally with your possessions or whatever you value.

Saturday, April 20 (Moon into Virgo, 8:10 p.m.)
Mars moves into your eleventh house today and stays there until May 31. You put a lot of energy into a favorite cause. You have the ability to generate interest and support for whatever you're pursuing. You can organize and take the lead. You work hard within a group, but take care to avoid getting overly aggressive with others.

Sunday, April 21 (Moon in Virgo)   The moon is in your third house today. You can be quite opinionated, especially when talking with siblings, other family members or neighbors. Try to stay in control of your emotions. You tend to be affected by matters from the past. Best to let it go.

Monday, April 22 (Moon in Virgo)   Take care of details now, especially related to your health. Exercise, and watch your diet. Stop worrying and fretting. Relax. Take time to write in a journal. You write from a deep place with lots of details and colorful descriptions. Dig deep for information, and take time to help others.

Tuesday, April 23 (Moon into Libra, 2:26 a.m.)
Trust your hunches; intuition is highlighted. You're inventive and make connections that others overlook. You get a fresh start, a new beginning. Don't be afraid to turn in a new direction. Stress originality.

Wednesday, April 24 (Moon in Libra)   With the moon in your fourth house today, it's a good day to stay at home or work there, if possible. Your intuition is highlighted. Spend time with your family and other loved ones. But also find time to focus inward in quiet meditation.

Thursday, April 25 (Moon into Scorpio, 5:27 a.m.) There's a lunar eclipse in your fifth house today. You gain insight into a matter dealing with romance, a creative project, or a child. If you feel that you need to take control of matters, make sure others are informed of what you're doing. Whatever the issue that comes up, it's a serious one.

Friday, April 26 (Moon in Scorpio) The moon is in your fifth house today. Creativity is emphasized, Cancer. Be yourself; be emotionally honest. In love there's greater emotional depth to a relationship now. You feel strongly attached to loved ones, particularly children. But eventually you need to let go.

Saturday, April 27 (Moon into Sagittarius, 6:33 a.m.) It's a number 5 day. Change and variety are highlighted. Think freedom, no restrictions. Find a new point of view that fits current circumstances and what you know now. Release old structures; get a new point of view. It's a good day to take a risk, experiment. Promote new ideas.

Sunday, April 28 (Moon in Sagittarius) The moon is in your sixth house today. It's a service day, Cancer. Others rely on you for help now. You improve, edit, and refine their work. Help them, but don't deny your own needs, and don't let your fears hold you back.

Monday, April 29 (Moon into Capricorn, 7:22 a.m.)
Look beneath the surface for the reasons others are shifting their points of view, "changing their tune." Knowledge is essential to success. You're a spy for your own cause today. Gather information, but don't make any absolute decisions until tomorrow. Make sure that you see things as they are, not as you wish them to be.

Tuesday, April 30 (Moon in Capricorn)   The moon is in your seventh house today. You communicate well with a spouse or partner, Cancer. It's all about working together. A contract or lawsuit could play a role. You get along well with others now, but it's a challenge to remain detached and objective.

MAY 2013

Wednesday, May 1 (Moon into Aquarius, 9:20 a.m.)
Mercury moves into your eleventh house, where it stays until May 15. You communicate well with friends and associates on a wide range of ideas. Your wishes and dreams take on new importance. You are open to getting help from anyone who has good ideas.

Thursday, May 2 (Moon in Aquarius)   Your experiences are more intense than usual. You have a strong sense of duty and feel obligated to fulfill your promises. Help others, but dance to your own tune. If you are planning on making a major purchase, make sure that you and your partner are in agreement. Otherwise you could encounter intense emotional resistance.

Friday, May 3 (Moon into Pisces, 1:26 p.m.)　It's a number 9 day. Complete what you've been working on, and get ready for something new. Consider ways to expand. Reflect on everything that has happened recently, and follow your intuitive nudges. A new cycle is about to begin.

Saturday, May 4 (Moon in Pisces)　The moon is in your ninth house today. You're a dreamer and a thinker. You may feel a need to get away now, a break from the usual routine. Pursue a new idea. Are you ready to plan a long trip?

Sunday, May 5 (Moon into Aries, 8:04 p.m.)　Use your intuition to get a sense of your day. Be kind and understanding. Cooperation and partnerships are highlighted. Don't make waves. Don't rush or show resentment; let things develop.

Monday, May 6 (Moon in Aries)　The moon is in your tenth house of profession and career today. You get a boost in your career now, an elevation in prestige. It's a good day for dealing with the public. But be careful not to cross the line between your private and professional lives.

Tuesday, May 7 (Moon in Aries)　It's a great time for initiating projects, launching new ideas, brainstorming. Be aware that emotions could be volatile. You're passionate but impatient. Imprint your style. Have an adventure; do something thrilling today.

Wednesday, May 8 (Moon into Taurus, 5:10 a.m.)
It's a number 5 day. Variety is the spice of life. Think freedom, no restrictions. Change and variety are highlighted now. Approach the day with an unconventional mindset. Release old structures; get a new point of view.

Thursday, May 9 (Moon in Taurus)   Venus moves into your twelfth house today, where it stays until June 2. There's nothing better now than solitude. Secrecy plays a role. You crave time alone to think things over, especially related to a romance. You might be wondering if someone special in your life was also a friend in a past life. Meanwhile, new opportunities could come your way through institutions, such as a hospital or government office.

Friday, May 10 (Moon into Gemini, 4:22 p.m.)
It's a number 7 day. Secrets, intrigue, confidential information play a role. Investigate activities taking place behind closed doors. You work best on your own today. Keep your own counsel. Knowledge is essential to success. Gather information, but don't make any absolute decisions until tomorrow.

Saturday, May 11 (Moon in Gemini)   The moon is in your twelfth house today. You might feel a need to withdraw and work behind the scenes. A troubling matter from the past could rise up now, or something related to your past or childhood could play a role. It's a great day for a mystical or spiritual discipline. Your intuition is heightened.

Sunday, May 12 (Moon in Gemini)   A change in scenery works to your advantage. Take a short trip out of town to visit family or friends. You're feeling creative and need to express yourself in writing. You see both sides of an issue.

Monday, May 13 (Moon into Cancer, 4:58 a.m.) You're at the top of your cycle today. Get out and meet new people, have new experiences, do something you've never done before. You could benefit from making some new friends and possibly encountering a romantic partner. You're inspired to turn your career in a new direction. Don't fear change.

Tuesday, May 14 (Moon in Cancer)   With the moon on your ascendant today, you're recharged for the remainder of the month, and this makes you more appealing to the public. You're physically vital, and relations with the opposite sex go well.

Wednesday, May 15 (Moon into Leo, 5:39 p.m.) Your attitude determines everything today. You communicate well. You're warm and receptive to what others say. Ease up on routines. Remain flexible. Enjoy the harmony, beauty, and pleasures of life.

Thursday, May 16 (Moon in Leo)   The moon is in your second house today, boding well for financial matters. Look at your priorities in handling your income. Take care of payments, and collect what's owed you. You equate your financial assets with emotional security now.

Friday, May 17 (Moon in Leo)   You're creative and passionate today, impulsive and honest. Drama and theatrics are highlighted. Be wild, imaginative. Be the person you always imagined you might be. Play with different personae. Romance feels majestic.

Saturday, May 18 (Moon into Virgo, 4:34 a.m.) It's another service day. Diplomacy is stressed. Be generous, tolerant, and diplomatic with those who complain and want more from you. Focus on making people happy. Do a good deed for someone. You offer advice and support.

Sunday, May 19 (Moon in Virgo)   The moon is in your third house today. No doubt you're running around today taking care of your everyday needs. Be especially careful when driving and talking on your cell phone. You make your point, and get your ideas across. However, control your emotions, especially when talking with siblings, other relatives, even neighbors.

Monday, May 20 (Moon into Libra, 12:08 p.m.) It's a number 8 day, your power day, Cancer. You pull off a financial coup. Expect a windfall. You're being watched by people in power. Be courageous. Be yourself; be honest. Remember that you're playing with power, so be careful not to hurt others.

Tuesday, May 21 (Moon in Libra)   The moon is in your fourth house today. Don't ignore domestic matters. If possible, stay home or work there. Find some quiet time for yourself to consider everything that has taken place recently. Family and other loved ones play a major role in your day.

Wednesday, May 22 (Moon into Scorpio, 3:56 p.m.)
You're at the top of your cycle again, Cancer. Trust your hunches; intuition is highlighted. Explore, discover, create. You're inventive and make connections that others overlook. You're determined and courageous today.

Thursday, May 23 (Moon in Scorpio)   The moon is in your fifth house today. You're emotionally in touch with your creative side now. There could be more involvement with kids. You feel strongly attached to loved ones, particularly children. You're more protective and nurturing, but try to avoid being too controlling. Pets could play a role, possibly involving a visit to the vet.

Friday, May 24 (Moon into Sagittarius, 4:50 p.m.)
It's a number 3 day. That means it's a good day to relax, enjoy yourself, recharge your batteries. Have fun today in preparation for tomorrow's discipline and focus. You can influence people now with your upbeat attitude. In romance you're an ardent and loyal lover.

Saturday, May 25 (Moon in Sagittarius)   There's a lunar eclipse in your sixth house today. You react emotionally to something going on in the workplace. You gain insight from the experience and see the big picture now, especially if it relates to your efforts to provide a service to others. You also could be dealing with a matter related to your health.

Sunday, May 26 (Moon into Capricorn, 4:29 p.m.)
Promote new ideas; follow your curiosity. Look for adventure. You're versatile and changeable. But be careful not to spread out and diversify too much. It's a good time to pursue self-employment. You're courageous and adaptable.

Monday, May 27 (Moon in Capricorn)   The moon is in your seventh house today. The focus turns to relationships, business and personal ones. Loved ones and partners play a role. A legal matter, possibly a marriage, comes to your attention now. You comprehend the nuances of a situation, but you've got some concerns.

Tuesday, May 28 (Moon into Aquarius, 4:49 p.m.)
It's a number 7 day, a mystery day. Look beneath the surface for the reasons others are shifting their points of view, "changing their tune." Knowledge is essential to success. You're a spy for your own cause today. Gather information, but don't make any absolute decisions until tomorrow. Make sure that you see things as they are, not as you wish them to be.

Wednesday, May 29 (Moon in Aquarius)   With the moon in your eighth house, Cancer, you could attract powerful people to you today. Your energy is more intense than usual, and drama plays a role. Your emotions could affect your feelings about belongings that you share with others. An interest in metaphysics or related rituals grabs your attention.

Thursday, May 30 (Moon into Pisces, 7:31 p.m.)
It's a number 9 day, and that means you should finish

whatever you started. Make room for something new. Clear your desk for tomorrow's new cycle, then look beyond the immediate. Strive for universal appeal.

Friday, May 31 (Moon in Pisces)   Mercury moves into your first house until June 27. You communicate well and are open to talking about your feelings. That's especially true if you're dealing with a health matter. With Mars moving into Gemini until July 13, you're mentally restless and looking for new information that could help you understand a matter from the past. Try not to get overly aggressive with others. Best to spend time working behind the scenes.

JUNE 2013

Saturday, June 1 (Moon in Pisces)   If you're feeling somewhat stressed and overworked, Cancer, you need to break out of your usual routine, or it could turn into a rut. Travel or higher education plays a role. Plan a trip or sign up for a seminar or workshop. A foreign country or person of foreign birth could play a role.

Sunday, June 2 (Moon into Aries, 1:34 a.m.)   Venus moves into your first house today, Cancer, and stays there until June 27. That suggests you're feeling very comfortable with yourself and your personal outlook. You're physically vital, and relations with the opposite sex are enhanced this month. You have a very strong desire to shine in front of the public.

Monday, June 3 (Moon in Aries)   The moon is in your tenth house today. Your professional life is energized now. You make a strong emotional commitment to your profession or to a role in public life. You gain recognition and prestige along with material success.

Tuesday, June 4 (Moon into Taurus, 10:55 a.m.) Cooperation is highlighted, and you work well with others. Your intuition focuses on relationships, either a new one that's developing or a current one. Don't make waves. Don't rush or show resentment; let things develop. Show your appreciation to others.

Wednesday, June 5 (Moon in Taurus) The moon is in your eleventh house today. Friends play an important role in your day. You find strength in numbers and meaning through friends and groups. You work for the common good, but keep an eye on your own wishes and dreams.

Thursday, June 6 (Moon into Gemini, 10:33 p.m.) Neptune goes retrograde in your ninth house today and stays that way until November 13. There could be some difficulties related to plans for higher education or long-distance travel. Something secretive and deceptive is going on. Move with care when discussing your plans. You get bogged down by any efforts to combine your plans with someone else's plans.

Friday, June 7 (Moon in Gemini) The moon is in your twelfth house today. It's a great day for a mystical or spiritual discipline. Your intuition is heightened. However, unconscious attitudes can be difficult now. So can relations with women. It's a good time for therapy and working behind the scenes.

Saturday, June 8 (Moon in Gemini)   There's a new moon in your twelfth house today. That means new opportunities come your way related to working on your own behind the scenes. It could relate to something from the past. Your feelings and memories play an important role. With Jupiter conjunct, you have an opportunity to expand whatever you're focused on.

Sunday, June 9 (Moon into Cancer, 11:17 a.m.) It's a number 7 day, a mystery day. You keep an eye on what's going on around you. You quickly come to a conclusion and wonder why others don't see what you see. You work best on your own today. Make sure that you see things as they are, not as you wish them to be. Knowledge is essential to success.

Monday, June 10 (Moon in Cancer)   The moon is in your first house today, Cancer. You're sensitive to other people's feelings. You feel moody one moment, happy the next, then withdrawn and sad. It's all about your emotional self. Your feelings and thoughts are aligned. You're dealing with your emotional self, the person you are becoming.

Tuesday, June 11 (Moon into Leo, 11:59 p.m.)   It's a number 9 day. It's a great time for completing projects and getting ready for something new. Clear up odds and ends. Take an inventory on where things are going in your life. It's time to make a donation to a worthy cause. Look beyond the present.

Wednesday, June 12 (Moon in Leo)   The moon is in your second house today. Expect emotional experiences related to money and your values. It's a good day for investments, but be practical. Don't make any major purchases now. You seek financial and domestic security, and you feel best surrounded by familiar objects.

Thursday, June 13 (Moon in Leo)   You're creative and passionate today, impulsive and honest. Dress boldly; showmanship is emphasized. Focus on advertising, publicity, publicizing yourself. Drama is highlighted, perhaps involving children.

Friday, June 14 (Moon into Virgo, 11:26 a.m.)   It's a number 3 day. You're innovative and creative and communicate well. You keep everyone in balance today. Your artistic talents are highlighted.

Saturday, June 15 (Moon in Virgo)   The moon is in your third house today. Your mental abilities are enhanced now, and you have an emotional need to reinvigorate your studies, especially regarding matters of the past. You're attracted to historical or archaeological studies. You write from a deep place today; it's a good day for journaling. Female relatives play a role.

Sunday, June 16 (Moon into Libra, 8:19 p.m.)   It's a number 5 day, and that means change and variety are highlighted. For example, a change of scenery would work to your advantage. You're seeking new horizons now. Approach the day with an unconventional mindset. Think freedom, no restrictions. Think outside the box. Take risks; experiment.

Monday, June 17 (Moon in Libra)   The moon is in your fourth house today. It's a good day to stay home, where you feel comfortable. The domestic scene plays a major role in your day. If possible, take the day off or work at home. You're feeling closer to your roots.

Tuesday, June 18 (Moon in Libra)   Romance is highlighted. Relationship issues figure prominently in your day. This is a great day to schedule an adventurous encounter with your significant other. Your friend is apt to be feeling as excited and enthusiastic about the day as you are. Attend a concert, art gallery, or museum opening. It's a day for feeding your creative juices.

Wednesday, June 19 (Moon into Scorpio, 1:39 a.m.) It's a number 8 day, your power day and your day to do it your way. You're in the power seat, so look for a power play. You have a chance to expand, to gain recognition, even fame and power. Be courageous. Be yourself; be honest.

Thursday, June 20 (Moon in Scorpio)   With the moon in your fifth house today, it's a good day to take a chance, experiment. Your creativity is emphasized, your originality highlighted. Be aware that your emotions tend to overpower your intellect now. Alternately, you are more protective and nurturing toward children.

Friday, June 21 (Moon into Sagittarius, 3:31 a.m.) It's a number 1 day, and you're at the top of your cycle,

Cancer. Get out and meet new people, have new experiences, do something you've never done before. Explore and discover. Creativity is highlighted. Express your opinions dynamically. In romance a flirtation turns more serious.

Saturday, June 22 (Moon in Sagittarius) The moon is in your sixth house today. It's a service day. Help others, but don't deny your own needs. Your personal health occupies your attention now. Maintain emotional balance.

Sunday, June 23 (Moon into Capricorn, 3:09 a.m.) There's a full moon in your seventh house today with Pluto conjunct. You reap what you've sown regarding partnerships. Contracts play a role. Your mind is active, and you ponder a relationship and where it's headed. Something very important culminates, and you are empowered.

Monday, June 24 (Moon in Capricorn) With the moon in your seventh house, the focus turns to relationships, both personal and business. You communicate well and get along with others now. You can fit in just about anywhere. You comprehend the nuances of a situation.

Tuesday, June 25 (Moon into Aquarius, 2:28 a.m.) Jupiter moves into your first house today, where it stays until mid-July 2014. So over the next year you should see opportunities for expansion in your personal life. Doors will open. You might go to college, graduate school, or law school. You also could get a manuscript published or get a job in publishing.

Wednesday, June 26 (Moon in Aquarius) Mercury goes retrograde in your first house, where it will stay until July 20. Personal matters could get confusing or delayed. Don't take anything for granted; check and recheck everything. Make sure that you communicate clearly so that others understand you.

Thursday, June 27 (Moon into Pisces, 3:33 a.m.) Venus moves into your second house today. You have a love of personal adornments now, whether that means jewelry, clothing, or even an upgrade in the vehicle you're driving. Wealth, whether you have it or are aspiring to it, makes you feel good. You can make money with your artistic abilities, and that's especially true over the next three weeks.

Friday, June 28 (Moon in Pisces) The moon is in your ninth house today. If you're feeling somewhat stressed and overworked, relax and take a deep breath. Plans for travel or higher education play a role. Sign up for a seminar or workshop. Study a foreign destination you want to visit, or take a lesson in a foreign language. A person of foreign birth could play a role.

Saturday, June 29 (Moon into Aries, 8:08 a.m.) It's a number 9 day and a good day to clear your desk and make room for the new, but don't start anything new until tomorrow. Spend some time in deep thought. Spiritual values arise. Use the day for reflection, expansion, and concluding projects. Strive for universal appeal.

Sunday, June 30 (Moon in Aries)   The moon is in your tenth house today. Professional concerns are on your mind this Sunday. You're thinking about a raise, bonus, or commendation. You're more responsive to the needs and moods of a group and the public in general. Be careful about blurring the boundary between your personal and professional lives.

JULY 2013

Monday, July 1 (Moon into Taurus, 4:44 p.m.)   It's a number 9 day, your day to finish up what you've been working on and get ready for something new. Take time to reflect on what you've been doing, and look for a way to expand. Visualize the future; set your goals, then make them so.

Tuesday, July 2 (Moon in Taurus)   The moon is in your eleventh house today. You get along better with friends and associates. Your sense of security is tied to your relationships. Work for the common good, but keep an eye on your own wishes and dreams.

Wednesday, July 3 (Moon in Taurus)   Health and physical activity are highlighted. It's a good time for gardening, cultivating ideas, doing practical things. While you maintain a common-sense, down-to-earth perspective on life, you also long for the good life with its material blessings.

Thursday, July 4 (Moon into Gemini, 4:23 a.m.)
Your imagination is keen now, and you communicate well. You're curious and inventive. You're warm and receptive to what others say. Enjoy the harmony, beauty, and pleasures of life. You have a strong sense of duty and feel obligated to fulfill your promises.

Friday, July 5 (Moon in Gemini) The moon is in your twelfth house today. You might feel a need to withdraw and work on your own. Think carefully before you act. There's a tendency now to undo all the positive actions you've taken. Avoid any self-destructive behavior. Be aware of hidden enemies.

Saturday, July 6 (Moon into Cancer, 5:14 p.m.)
It's a number 2 day. That means partnerships and cooperation are highlighted. Help comes through friends or loved ones, especially a partner. Don't make waves. Don't rush or show resentment; let things develop. You could be undergoing some soul-searching related to a relationship now.

Sunday, July 7 (Moon in Cancer) Saturn goes direct in your fifth house today. Issues related to a creative project or to children in your life are resolved. Also, difficulties related to a romance or relationship are over. You need to enhance the base or foundation of a creative project or relationship.

Monday, July 8 (Moon in Cancer) There's a new moon in your first house today, and four other planets are also in Cancer! That means the focus is on your personal life, your health and emotions. You're dealing with the person you are becoming. New opportunities come your way now. You're feeling recharged and ready to go. You're physically vital, and relations with the opposite sex go well.

Tuesday, July 9 (Moon into Leo, 5:48 a.m.) It's a number 8 day, your power day. Business discussions go well. You attract financial success. Open your mind to a new approach that could bring in big bucks. You have a chance to expand, to gain recognition, even fame and power.

Wednesday, July 10 (Moon in Leo) The moon is in your second house today. You tend to react emotionally now to an event in your life related to money or your values. You identify emotionally with your possessions or whatever you value. Look at your priorities in handling your income. Watch your spending.

Thursday, July 11 (Moon into Virgo, 5:12 p.m.) It's a number 1 day, and you're at the top of your cycle. You take the lead in something new and get a fresh start, a new beginning. Stress originality. You attract creative people now and avoid those with closed minds. Trust your hunches.

Friday, July 12 (Moon in Virgo) The moon is in your third house today. You write from a deep place today; it's a good day for journaling. Be aware that your thinking may be unduly influenced by things from the past. You could be visiting with relatives or siblings or spending time in the community with your neighbors. You accept an invitation to a social event.

Saturday, July 13 (Moon in Virgo)   With Mars moving into your first house today, you're quite outgoing and assertive now, letting others know exactly what you think and how you feel. Others see you as ambitious. Your feelings and thoughts are aligned.

Sunday, July 14 (Moon into Libra, 2:41 a.m.)   It's a number 4 day. Tear down the old in order to rebuild. Be methodical and thorough. Take care of your obligations. Your organizational skills are highlighted. You tend to stay with the tried and true. It's not a day for experimentation or new approaches.

Monday, July 15 (Moon in Libra)   The moon is in your fourth house. You're dealing with the foundations of who you are and who you are becoming. Retreat to a private place for meditation. It's a good day for dream recall. Change a bad habit. A parent plays a role.

Tuesday, July 16 (Moon into Scorpio, 9:25 a.m.) It's a number 6 day, a service day. Adjust to the needs of loved ones. Diplomacy wins the day. Focus on making people happy. Be sympathetic, kind, and compassionate. You serve, teach, and guide. But know when to say enough is enough.

Wednesday, July 17 (Moon in Scorpio)   Uranus goes retrograde in your tenth house today and stays that way until December 17. That means you might be doing some soul-searching about your career goals. You could be getting flashes of inspiration related to what you really want to do. Matters are somewhat unpredictable over the next few months. Avoid going to extremes. Pushing yourself too hard could result in accidents. Watch your step! Be careful when talking on your cell and driving, Cancer.

Thursday, July 18 (Moon into Sagittarius, 12:55 p.m.) It's your power day, Cancer, and your day to play it your way. Think big and act big! You can go far with your plans and achieve financial success, especially if you open your mind to a new approach.

Friday, July 19 (Moon in Sagittarius) The moon is in your sixth house today, Cancer. People look to you for help. You can improve whatever others are working on. Keep your resolutions about exercise, and watch your diet. Attend to details related to your health. Make a doctor or dentist appointment.

Saturday, July 20 (Moon into Capricorn, 1:40 p.m.) Mercury goes direct in your first house today. That means any confusion, miscommunication, and delays that you've been experiencing, especially related to a health or personal matter, recede into the past. Things move more smoothly now. You get your ideas across.

Sunday, July 21 (Moon in Capricorn) The moon is in your seventh house today. You get along well with others now. You can fit in just about anywhere. Loved ones and partners are more important than usual. Take time to consider how others see you. You're in the public eye.

Monday, July 22 (Moon into Aquarius, 1:08 p.m.) Venus moves into your third house today, and that means you get along well with your family, because you don't want to argue. You're also more willing to compromise over the next three weeks. With the full moon in your eighth house, you have a better understanding of matters such as a mortgage, taxes, credit cards, or insurance. You could also gain insight related to a metaphysical subject such as astrology, ghosts, or past lives.

Tuesday, July 23 (Moon in Aquarius)   The moon is in your eighth house of shared resources and investments today. Your experiences are more intense than usual. You have a strong sense of duty and feel obligated to fulfill your promises. Security is an important issue with you right now. As yesterday, it's a good day for dealing with mortgages, insurance, and investments.

Wednesday, July 24 (Moon into Pisces, 1:23 p.m.) It's a number 5 day. You're versatile and changeable now, but be careful not to spread yourself too thin. Release old structures; get a new point of view. Take a risk; experiment. Approach the day with an unconventional mindset.

Thursday, July 25 (Moon in Pisces)   The moon is in your ninth house today. Your mind is active, and you yearn for new experiences, a break from the routine, a change from the status quo. You can create positive change through your ideas now. A publishing project takes off. Publicity and advertising are emphasized.

Friday, July 26 (Moon into Aries, 4:30 p.m.)   It's your mystery day, Cancer. You could be dealing with confidential information and intrigue. Dig deep for information. Express your desires, but avoid self-deception. Make sure that you see things as they are, not as you wish them to be.

Saturday, July 27 (Moon in Aries)   The moon is in your tenth house today. Business dealings are highlighted on this Saturday. It's a good day for sales and dealing with the public. You get along well with fellow workers. Avoid any emotional displays in public.

Sunday, July 28 (Moon into Taurus, 11:44 p.m.) Finish what you started. Visualize the future; set your goals, then make them so. Look beyond the immediate. Get ready for something new, but don't start anything until tomorrow. Strive for universal appeal.

Monday, July 29 (Moon in Taurus)   The moon is in your eleventh house today. You get along better with friends and associates, who play an important role in your day. Focus on your wishes and dreams. Examine your overall goals. Those goals should be an expression of who you are. You get a fresh start.

Tuesday, July 30 (Moon in Taurus)   Health and physical activity are highlighted. It's a good time for gardening, cultivating ideas, doing practical things. Use common sense, and take a down-to-earth perspective on whatever you're doing.

Wednesday, July 31 (Moon into Gemini, 10:42 a.m.) Play your hunches now. Have fun today in preparation for tomorrow's discipline and focus. Make time to listen to others. You can influence people with your upbeat attitude. Take time to relax, enjoy yourself, recharge your batteries.

AUGUST 2013

Thursday, August 1 (Moon in Gemini)   The moon is in your twelfth house today. It's a good day to withdraw from the action and keep to yourself. Work on a solo project. Keep your feelings secret. Be aware that relations with women can be difficult now. Things affecting you from the past could surface.

Friday, August 2 (Moon into Cancer, 11:30 p.m.) It's a number 2 day. Don't make waves. Don't rush or show resentment; let things develop. Cooperation is highlighted. Use your intuition to get a sense of your day.

Saturday, August 3 (Moon in Cancer)   The moon is on your ascendant today. That means the way you see yourself now is the way others see you. You're recharged for the month ahead, and this makes you more appealing to the public. You're physically vital, and you can expect relations with the opposite sex to go well.

Sunday, August 4 (Moon in Cancer)   The moon is in your first house today. You're dealing with the person you're becoming. Your self-awareness and appearance take on new meaning. It's all about your emotional self and your health. Your moods can shift from ebullient to sad and then back again in a short time.

Monday, August 5 (Moon into Leo, 11:58 a.m.)
Get ready for change. It's a good day to experiment and let go of old structures. Variety is the spice of life. Release old structures. Promote new ideas, and follow your curiosity. Freedom of thought and action is key.

Tuesday, August 6 (Moon in Leo) The new moon is in your second house today, Cancer, and that means opportunities come your way related to money-making ideas. Financial matters work to your advantage now. With Uranus trine to the moon, you could be in for some pleasant surprises.

Wednesday, August 7 (Moon into Virgo, 10:58 p.m.)
You take a journey into the unknown today. You could be dealing with confidential information and intrigue. Dig deep for information. Express your desires, but avoid self-deception. Make sure that you see things as they are, not as you wish them to be.

Thursday, August 8 (Moon in Virgo) Mercury moves into your second house. There's lots of mental stimulation now regarding finances. You communicate your fresh ideas related to money-making projects. You also discuss your insights into your values or whatever you value.

Friday, August 9 (Moon in Virgo) The moon is in your third house today. Get your ideas across as you go about your everyday activities. Take what you've learned recently, and tell others about it. But avoid getting overly emotional, especially when dealing with neighbors or relatives.

Saturday, August 10 (Moon into Libra, 8:09 a.m.)
You're at the top of your cycle again, Cancer. Trust your hunches today. You get a fresh start, a new beginning. You're inventive and make connections that others overlook. Don't be afraid to turn in a new direction.

Sunday, August 11 (Moon in Libra)   The moon is in your fourth house today. Spend time with your family and loved ones. Stick close to home, if possible. You could be dealing with parents now. You're dealing with the foundations of who you are and who you are becoming.

Monday, August 12 (Moon into Scorpio, 3:19 p.m.)
Your attitude determines everything today. Ease up on routines, and spread your good news. You communicate well. You're warm and receptive to what others say. Remain flexible, and enjoy the harmony, beauty, and pleasures of life.

Tuesday, August 13 (Moon in Scorpio)   Romance and sex for pleasure are highlighted. Your emotions tend to overpower your intellect now, and you're in touch with your creative side. You feel strongly attached to loved ones, particularly children.

Wednesday, August 14 (Moon into Sagittarius, 8:05 p.m.)   It's a number 5 day. Freedom of thought and action is highlighted. Change your perspective. Approach the day with an unconventional mindset. Promote new ideas; follow your curiosity. You can overcome obstacles with ease.

Thursday, August 15 (Moon in Sagittarius) The moon is in your sixth house today, Cancer. Keep up with your exercise regimen, and watch your diet. Attend to details related to your health; make a doctor or dentist appointment. Your personal health occupies your attention now. Help others, but don't deny your own needs.

Friday, August 16 (Moon into Capricorn, 10:26 p.m.) Venus moves into your fourth house today. Stay home this evening for a romantic interlude with your sweetheart. Domestic matters are highlighted. Take time to beautify your home with something new. You feel a close and loving tie to your roots.

Saturday, August 17 (Moon in Capricorn) Yesterday's energy flows into your Saturday. You feel a strong desire to work with a partner now. You don't feel complete unless you and your partner or spouse are in tune. Avoid conflicts; go with the flow.

Sunday, August 18 (Moon into Aquarius, 11:07 p.m.) It's a number 9 day. Finish what you started. Visualize the future; set your goals, then make them so. Look beyond the immediate. Get ready for something new. Strive for universal appeal.

Monday, August 19 (Moon in Aquarius) The moon in your eighth house can affect your feelings about your belongings as well as things that you share with others, such as a spouse. You have a strong sense of duty and feel obligated to fulfill your promises. Security is an important issue with you right now.

Tuesday, August 20 (Moon into Pisces, 11:44 p.m.)
With the full moon in your eighth house, you gain insight into a matter related to shared resources, an inheritance, or an insurance policy. You also better understand a metaphysical subject, such as life after death or astrology.

Wednesday, August 21 (Moon in Pisces) The feeling of security is an important issue with you right now. Your experiences are more intense than usual. You have a strong sense of duty and feel obligated to fulfill your promises. It's a good time to get involved in a cause aimed at improving life for large numbers of people.

Thursday, August 22 (Moon in Pisces) Imagination is highlighted. Watch for psychic events, synchronicities. Keep track of your dreams, including your daydreams. Ideas are ripe. It's a time for deep healing and inspiration.

Friday, August 23 (Moon into Aries, 2:13 a.m.)
It's a number 5 day. Change and variety are highlighted. Think freedom; think outside the box. Eliminate any restrictions. Your creativity, personal grace, and magnetism are highlighted.

Saturday, August 24 (Moon in Aries) The moon is in your tenth house today. Business or career matters are highlighted on this Saturday. You gain an elevation in prestige. You're more emotional and warm toward coworkers. You're also in the public eye now, so avoid any emotional displays. Be careful about crossing the line between your personal and professional lives.

Sunday, August 25 (Moon into Taurus, 8:14 a.m.) It's a number 7 day, your mystery day, Cancer. You work best on your own today. Knowledge is essential to success. Gather information, but don't make any absolute decisions until tomorrow. Go with the flow. Express your desires, but avoid self-deception.

Monday, August 26 (Moon in Taurus)   The moon is in your eleventh house today. Friends play an important role in your day, especially Scorpio and Pisces. While it was better for you to work on your own yesterday, today you find strength in numbers. You find meaning through friends and groups, especially a group of like-minded people working for the common good.

Tuesday, August 27 (Moon into Gemini, 6:08 p.m.) Mars moves into your sixth house today and stays there until October 15. You work hard to get things done. Be aware that coworkers might get annoyed by your aggressive behavior on the job. Control your temper. Don't be so concerned about details and getting everything perfect. It will all work out.

Wednesday, August 28 (Moon in Gemini)   The moon is in your twelfth house today. Unconscious attitudes can be difficult. Best to keep your feelings secret. It's a great day for a mystical or spiritual discipline. Your intuition is heightened.

Thursday, August 29 (Moon in Gemini) A change of scenery works to your advantage today. Contact with siblings, other relatives, or neighbors offers an opportunity to exchange new information. You see two sides of an issue now, Cancer. Get out, have fun, flirt.

Friday, August 30 (Moon into Cancer, 6:33 a.m.) It's a number 3 day. You can influence people now with your upbeat attitude. You're innovative and creative and communicate well. Enjoy the harmony, beauty, and pleasures of life. Remain flexible, warm, and receptive.

Saturday, August 31 (Moon in Cancer) The moon is in your first house today. You're feeling particularly sensitive. You're easily influenced by what others say, and you're also responsive to the way others relate to you. You're malleable and tend to change your mind on a whim now. You're dealing with your emotional self, the person you are becoming.

SEPTEMBER 2013

Sunday, September 1 (Moon into Leo, 7:02 p.m.) It's a number 2 day. That means that cooperation and partnership are highlighted again. There's a new beginning now, or a new opportunity arises. Your intuition focuses on relationships. Don't make waves. Don't rush or show resentment; let things develop.

Monday, September 2 (Moon in Leo) The moon is in your second house today. You identify emotionally with your values now or whatever you value. You tend to equate your assets with emotional security. You feel best when surrounded by familiar objects, especially in your home. It's not the objects themselves that are important, but the feelings and memories you associate with them.

Tuesday, September 3 (Moon in Leo) You're at center stage today, Cancer. Theatrics and drama are highlighted. Strut your stuff; showmanship is emphasized. You're impulsive and honest. Romance and love play a role.

Wednesday, September 4 (Moon into Virgo, 5:45 a.m.) It's a number 5 day. Change and variety are highlighted now. Think freedom, no restrictions. Change your perspective. Approach the day with an unconventional mindset. Release old structures; get a new point of view. A change of scenery would work to your advantage.

Thursday, September 5 (Moon in Virgo) There's a new moon in your third house today. New opportunities come your way related to your everyday world. You can expand whatever you're doing. You gain a better understanding of the details, especially those that relate to the past.

Friday, September 6 (Moon into Libra, 2:14 p.m.) It's your mystery day, Cancer. You become aware of confidential information, secret meetings, things happening behind closed doors. You investigate like a detective solving a mystery. Dig deep and gather information, but don't act on what you learn until tomorrow.

Saturday, September 7 (Moon in Libra)   The moon is in your fourth house, a comfortable place for you, Cancer. It's a good day to take off and stay home or work at home. Find time for a home-repair project. You could be dealing with parents now. You feel a close tie to your roots.

Sunday, September 8 (Moon into Scorpio, 8:45 p.m.) It's a number 9 day. Clear your desk for tomorrow's new cycle. Accept what comes your way now, but don't start anything new today. Use the day for reflection, expansion, and concluding projects.

Monday, September 9 (Moon in Scorpio)   Mercury moves into your fourth house today. There's strong mental activity in the home now, a high priority on learning. Home schooling a child is a possibility. Alternately, you're thinking a lot about your home, selling it or remodeling some aspect of it.

Tuesday, September 10 (Moon in Scorpio)   You're emotionally in touch with your creative side now. There's also greater depth in a love relationship, and more involvement with children and pets. You're emotionally tied to your children, but make sure you allow them room to grow.

Wednesday, September 11 (Moon into Sagittarius, 1:36 a.m.)   Venus moves into your fifth house today. That means you're very attractive to the opposite sex now and thrive on romantic attention. You also would enjoy visiting a museum or art gallery over the next three weeks. Others find you charming and easy-going.

Thursday, September 12 (Moon in Sagittarius) The moon is in your sixth house today. It's another service day, Cancer. If someone in your home environment could use your advice, be there for that person. Help others, but dance to your own tune. You improve, edit, and refine their work.

Friday, September 13 (Moon into Capricorn, 4:56 a.m.) Change and variety are highlighted now. Think freedom; think outside the box. Your creativity, personal grace, and magnetism are highlighted. Get ready for changes. Promote new ideas; follow your curiosity. Look for adventure.

Saturday, September 14 (Moon in Capricorn) The moon is in your seventh house today. You get along well with others now. You can fit in just about anywhere. Loved ones and partners are more important than usual. You comprehend the nuances of a situation, but it's difficult to go with the flow. Be careful that others don't manipulate your feelings.

Sunday, September 15 (Moon into Aquarius, 7:06 a.m.) It's a number 7 day. Knowledge is essential to success. You investigate, analyze, or simply observe what's going on. Gather information, but don't make any absolute decisions until tomorrow. Go with the flow.

Monday, September 16 (Moon in Aquarius)   The moon is in your eighth house today. Your experiences are more intense than usual. You could be exploring a metaphysical matter, such as life after death or psychic abilities. Your intuition is strong. Security is an important issue now. You could be managing resources that you share with others.

Tuesday, September 17 (Moon into Pisces, 8:59 a.m.) It's a number 9 day. Clear up odds and ends. Accept what comes your way, but don't start anything new. It's all part of a cycle. Use the day for reflection, expansion, and concluding projects. Strive for universal appeal.

Wednesday, September 18 (Moon in Pisces)   The moon is in your ninth house today, the home of higher learning. You're full of ideas now on matters such as philosophy or religion, the law or publishing. You also have a strong interest in foreign travel or a foreign nation. It's a good time to look to the big picture, Cancer. Break away from your routine or the usual way you think about things.

Thursday, September 19 (Moon into Aries, 11:58 a.m.)   There's a full moon in your ninth house today. Now you have an opportunity to clarify and expand what you were working on or thinking about yesterday. You gain a better understanding of a matter related to higher education or long-distance travel.

Friday, September 20 (Moon in Aries)   Pluto goes direct in your seventh house today, where it will remain until 2024. That releases more energy for a partnership or marriage. You could be dealing with a new contract or contracts. You're moving forward and outward. A partnership plays a role. Keep in mind that Pluto transforms everything that is not needed.

Saturday, September 21 (Moon into Taurus, 5:34 p.m.)   It's a good day to get organized. Clean out your garage, attic, or closet. Tear down the old in order to rebuild. Be methodical and thorough. Missing papers are found. Revise and rewrite. You're building a creative base.

Sunday, September 22 (Moon in Taurus)   The moon is in your eleventh house today. Friends play an important role in your day, especially Scorpio and Pisces. You work well with others, especially in a group. Focus on your wishes and dreams. Examine your overall goals, and make sure that they're still an expression of who you are.

Monday, September 23 (Moon in Taurus)   You're feeling strong-willed today. Be aware that you might be somewhat stubborn and resistant to change. Health and physical activity are highlighted. It's a good time for cultivating ideas, but make sure that they're practical.

Tuesday, September 24 (Moon into Gemini, 2:35 a.m.)   It's a number 7 day. Secrets, intrigue, confidential information play a role today. You might feel best working on your own. You investigate, analyze, or simply observe what's going on now. You quickly come to a conclusion and wonder why others don't see what you see. It's best to hold off on making any final decisions for a couple of days.

Wednesday, September 25 (Moon in Gemini) The moon is in your twelfth house today. Think carefully before you act. There's a tendency now to undo all the positive actions you've taken. Avoid any self-destructive behavior. Be aware of hidden enemies. You might feel a need to withdraw and work on your own.

Thursday, September 26 (Moon into Cancer, 2:25 p.m.) Look beyond the immediate. Finish what you started. Make room for something new. Take an inventory on where things are going in your life. It's a good day to make a donation to a worthy cause.

Friday, September 27 (Moon in Cancer) With the moon in your first house today, Cancer, your thoughts and emotions are aligned. You could feel somewhat moody, shifting from happy one moment, sad the next, then back again. You're dealing with your self-awareness, your appearance, and the person you are becoming.

Saturday, September 28 (Moon in Cancer) The moon is on your ascendant today, and you're re-charged for the month ahead. This makes you more appealing to the public. The way you see yourself now is the way others see you. Your face is in front of the public now. You're restless, impulsive, and inquisitive. Worldviews arise.

Sunday, September 29 (Moon into Leo, 2:58 a.m.)
Mercury moves into your fifth house today. You communicate well, especially with a lover. You get your message across. Alternately, you could feel strongly about a creative project you're working on or about a child or children.

Monday, September 30 (Moon in Leo)　The moon is in your second house today. Money and material goods are important to you now and give you a sense of security. You identify emotionally with your possessions or whatever you value. Watch your spending.

OCTOBER 2013

Tuesday, October 1 (Moon into Virgo, 1:53 p.m.)
Your attitude determines everything today. Spread your good news, and take time to listen to others. You will find that if you allow yourself free time to pursue a creative project, then your spirits will soar as will your productivity.

Wednesday, October 2 (Moon in Virgo)　The moon is in your third house today. As you go about your everyday life, look to the past for clues about what's coming up in the near future. Your mental abilities are strong now, and you have an emotional need to reinvigorate your studies, especially regarding matters of the past. You also could be getting involved in a challenging mental activity, such as on-line gaming, a debate, or a game of chess, anything that challenges your mental prowess.

Thursday, October 3 (Moon into Libra, 10:00 p.m.)
You're restless and looking for change, a new perspective. You're versatile and changeable, but be careful not to overcommit yourself now. Take risks, experiment, and pursue a new idea. Freedom of thought and action is key.

Friday, October 4 (Moon in Libra)   There's a new moon in your fourth house today. You're dealing with the foundations of who you are and who you are becoming. You get a fresh start on your domestic life. That could mean a move or a renovation of your home. Alternately, you revitalize contact with your roots, either parents or friends from childhood.

Saturday, October 5 (Moon in Libra)   Yesterday's energy flows into your Saturday with the focus on the domestic scene. You feel close to your family, your home, your property. Work on a home-repair project. Beautify your home. But also take time to retreat to a special private place for meditation.

Sunday, October 6 (Moon into Scorpio, 3:33 a.m.)
It's your power day and your day to play it your way. Be flexible, and look for a new approach that could bring in big bucks. Remember you're playing with power, so be careful not to hurt others.

Monday, October 7 (Moon in Scorpio)   Venus moves into your sixth house today. You take great pleasure in the workplace this month. You get along well with coworkers and offer your assistance. You also feel good about your health situation and your diet.

Tuesday, October 8 (Moon into Sagittarius, 7:22 a.m.)   It's a number 1 day. You're at the top of your cycle. Get out and meet new people, have new experiences. Do something that you've never done before. In romance something new is developing. Stress originality. Refuse to deal with people who have closed minds.

Wednesday, October 9 (Moon in Sagittarius)   The moon is in your sixth house today. It's another service day. However, you could be feeling sensitive now and emotionally down. Help others where you can, but avoid falling into a martyr syndrome. Take time to exercise, and eat healthy meals. Get ready for a fun day tomorrow.

Thursday, October 10 (Moon into Capricorn, 10:18 a.m.)   Take time to relax, enjoy yourself, recharge your batteries. You can influence people now with your upbeat attitude. Play your hunches. In business dealings, diversify now. Insist on all the information, not just bits and pieces.

Friday, October 11 (Moon in Capricorn)   The moon is in your seventh house today. You get along well with others now. You can fit in just about anywhere. Loved ones and partners are more important than usual. You focus on how the public relates to you. You feel a need to be accepted. You're looking for security, but you have a hard time going with the flow.

Saturday, October 12 (Moon into Aquarius, 1:00 p.m.) Approach the day with an unconventional mindset. Experiment; promote new ideas. You're feeling versatile and changeable today, but be careful not to diversify too much. You'll be in a hurry all day, so watch your step.

Sunday, October 13 (Moon in Aquarius) The moon is in your eighth house today. You could attract the attention of powerful people. Your experiences could be more intense than usual. Matters related to shared belongings, investments, taxes, or insurance could play a role. A metaphysical subject, such as life after death or astrology, catches your attention.

Monday, October 14 (Moon into Pisces, 4:06 p.m.) Get ready for a journey into the unknown. Secrets, intrigue, confidential information play a role. Knowledge is essential to success. Gather information, but avoid making any absolute decisions for the time being. You work best on your own today.

Tuesday, October 15 (Moon in Pisces) Mars moves into your third house today. You're more aggressive in pursuing your everyday activities over the next three weeks. You could be confronting a matter from the past. Be aware of your tendencies during this time to act more confrontational than usual, Cancer. That's especially true when dealing with siblings, other relatives, or neighbors.

Wednesday, October 16 (Moon into Aries, 8:19 p.m.) It's a number 9 day. Complete a project now. Make room for something new. Visualize the future; set your goals, then make them so. Strive for universal appeal. Spiritual values surface.

Thursday, October 17 (Moon in Aries)   The moon is in your tenth house today. It's a good day for dealing with the public, Cancer. Your thoughts and especially your feelings are more exposed. You're more responsive to the needs and moods of a group and the public in general. You gain an elevation in prestige.

Friday, October 18 (Moon in Aries)   There's a lunar eclipse in your tenth house today. That means you react emotionally to an event related to your professional life. Whatever is happening, you gain insight that can help you move ahead in your career.

Saturday, October 19 (Moon into Taurus, 2:28 a.m.) It's a number 3 day. Your charm and wit are appreciated. You're curious and inventive now. Take time to relax and get your batteries recharged. In romance you are ardent and feeling loyal to your partner.

Sunday, October 20 (Moon in Taurus)   The moon is in your eleventh house today. Friends play an important role in your day, especially Pisces and Scorpio. You find strength in numbers. Focus on your wishes and dreams. Examine your overall goals. Those goals should be an expression of who you are.

Monday, October 21 (Moon into Gemini, 11:15 a.m.)   Mercury goes retrograde in your fifth house today and stays that way until November 10. That means you can expect some delays and glitches in communication over the next three weeks, especially related to children or a creative project. Expect some confusion in dealings with a romantic partner as well.

He or she might misinterpret your intentions. It's best to relax and control your emotional reactions to situations now.

Tuesday, October 22 (Moon in Gemini) The moon is in your twelfth house today, Cancer. Unconscious attitudes can be difficult. Keep your feelings secret. You might feel a need to withdraw and work on your own. Take time to reflect and meditate. It's a great time for pursuing a spiritual discipline.

Wednesday, October 23 (Moon into Cancer, 10:37 p.m.) It's a number 7 day. Secrets, intrigue, confidential information play a role. Gather information, but don't make any absolute decisions until tomorrow. You investigate, analyze, or simply observe what's going on now. You quickly come to a conclusion and wonder why others don't see what you see. You detect deception and recognize insincerity with ease.

Thursday, October 24 (Moon in Cancer) The moon is in your first house today, Cancer. Domestic matters play a big role in your day, especially related to your feelings about your home life. It's all about your emotional self. Your thoughts and feelings are aligned. Self-awareness and appearance are important now.

Friday, October 25 (Moon in Cancer) With the moon in your first house and on your ascendant, you get your batteries recharged. You're physically vital, Cancer, and get along well with the opposite sex. You're also malleable and easily change your mind now. You're restless and uncertain which direction to proceed.

Saturday, October 26 (Moon into Leo, 11:13 a.m.)
You're at the top of your cycle again. Be independent,
creative, and refuse to be discouraged by naysayers.
Take the lead, get a fresh start, a new beginning. Don't
be afraid to turn in a new direction. Trust your
hunches; intuition is highlighted.

Sunday, October 27 (Moon in Leo)   The moon is
in your second house today. Finances and money issues take center stage now, Cancer. You identify emotionally with your possessions or whatever you value.
Watch your spending. You feel best when surrounded
by familiar objects, especially in your home environment. It's not the objects themselves that are important, but the feelings and memories you associate with
them. Put off making any major purchases now.

Monday, October 28 (Moon into Virgo, 10:45 p.m.)
Your charm and wit are appreciated. You're curious
and inventive. Take time to relax and get your batteries recharged. In romance you are ardent and feeling
loyal to your partner. The social energy of the day is
warm and welcoming.

Tuesday, October 29 (Moon in Virgo)   The moon
is in your third house today, Cancer. You get your
ideas across, but try not to get too emotional, especially with siblings and neighbors. A female relative
plays an important role. Follow your hunches. You
write from a deep place.

Wednesday, October 30 (Moon in Virgo)   Take
care of details now; read the fine print. You might find

that your colleagues are speeding ahead of you while you are stuck rechecking, revising, or editing. Take your time, and proceed at your own pace. Don't let the pace of others intimidate you. Also, pay attention to any health or diet issue.

Thursday, October 31 (Moon into Libra, 7:22 a.m.) It's a number 6 day. Service to others is the theme of the day. Offer your advice and support. Diplomacy wins the way. Be sympathetic and kind, generous and tolerant.

NOVEMBER 2013

Friday, November 1 (Moon in Libra)   You're busy keeping your mind occupied with new information. Take what you know, and share it with others. Your communications with others are subjective, so keep conscious control of your emotions when speaking. Your thinking is unduly influenced by things of the past.

Saturday, November 2 (Moon into Scorpio, 1:35 p.m.)   A change of scenery would work to your advantage. You could be moving to a new location. You can overcome obstacles with ease. It's a good time for travel, adventure, and meeting new people. You're seeking new horizons, but you tend to lack order and discipline.

Sunday, November 3—Daylight Saving Time Ends (Moon in Scorpio)   There's a solar eclipse in your fifth house today. That means new opportunities come your way related to a creative project that could involve children. With four planets also in Scorpio, everything is enhanced—for better or worse—especially your personal health. It's the beginning or end of something that could be related to a romantic alliance.

Monday, November 4 (Moon into Sagittarius, 3:14 p.m.)   It's a number 7 day. Secrets, intrigue, confidential information play a role. You investigate, analyze, or simply observe what's going on now. You quickly come to a conclusion and wonder why others don't see what you see. You detect deception and recognize insincerity with ease. Gather information, but don't make any absolute decisions until tomorrow.

Tuesday, November 5 (Moon in Sagittarius)   Venus moves into your seventh house today. For the rest of the month you'll get along well with a partner in either a personal or business relationship. You see eye to eye and you feel close to each other. A contract could be involved, and you gain in status as a result.

Wednesday, November 6 (Moon into Capricorn, 4:44 p.m.)   It's a number 9 day, a good day to complete a project and get ready for a fresh start. Accept what comes your way now. It's all part of a cycle. Use the day for reflection, expansion, and concluding projects. Don't start anything new today.

Thursday, November 7 (Moon in Capricorn)   With Jupiter going direct in your first house today, you have an opportunity to expand your personal life into new areas. Your thoughts and emotions are aligned, and you see the big picture. You feel that anything is possible now.

Friday, November 8 (Moon into Aquarius, 6:31 p.m.)   It's a number 2 day. Cooperation and partnerships are highlighted. Your intuition focuses on relationships. You're diplomatic and capable of fixing whatever has gone wrong. You excel in working with others. You're playing the role of the visionary today.

Saturday, November 9 (Moon in Aquarius)   The moon is in your eighth house today. You feel a need to help others, but your own security is also important. You could be managing other people's resources now. You take a renewed interest in a metaphysical subject, such as astrology.

Sunday, November 10 (Moon into Pisces, 9:37 p.m.) Mercury goes direct in your fifth house today. Misunderstandings and miscommunication with a romantic partner recede into the past. Also, you can move ahead with a creative project. You get along better with any children in your life. The delays and confusion are over.

Monday, November 11 (Moon in Pisces)   The moon is in your ninth house today, the home of higher learning. You communicate well now. Ideas and philosophies are important, especially those that help you advance in your plans, Cancer. It's a good day to prepare for a trip or sign up for a seminar or workshop. A foreign country or person of foreign birth could play a role. Publicity and advertising are emphasized.

Tuesday, November 12 (Moon in Pisces)   It's a good day to escape from the usual routine and the drudgery, Cancer. You're a dreamer *and* a thinker today, but now you're ready for action. You're restless and yearn for a new experience, and now you have the energy to follow through. Plan a long trip. Sign up for a workshop or seminar.

Wednesday, November 13 (Moon into Aries, 2:40 a.m.)   With Neptune going direct in your ninth house today, you could be working on your belief system. You're looking for the ideal situation in higher education or long-distance travel. It's a great time for initiating projects, launching new ideas, brainstorming.

Thursday, November 14 (Moon in Aries)   With the moon in your tenth house today, you communicate your feelings well to coworkers, who are sympathetic. You're looking for a raise or an advancement; you know you deserve it. Your life is more public now. It's a good day for sales, dealing with the public.

Friday, November 15 (Moon into Taurus, 9:50 a.m.) Complete a project now, and take an inventory on where things are going in your life. Clear your desk for tomorrow's new cycle. Accept what comes your way, but don't start anything new until tomorrow.

Saturday, November 16 (Moon in Taurus)   The moon is in your eleventh house today. You work well with group of like-minded individuals. You find strength in numbers. At the same time your individuality is stressed. Focus on your wishes and dreams. Examine your overall goals. Those goals should be an expression of who you are. Social consciousness plays a role in your day.

Sunday, November 17 (Moon into Gemini, 7:08 p.m.) There's a full moon in your eleventh house today. Friends play an important role. You reap what you've sown related to your wishes and dreams. You gain a better understanding of your relationships with friends and associates. You work well with a group of like-minded people.

Monday, November 18 (Moon in Gemini) The moon is in your twelfth house today. Think carefully before you act or speak. Consider: is it kind, is it true, is it necessary? If you're not careful, there's a tendency now to undo all the positive actions you've taken. You might feel a need to withdraw. Take time to reflect and meditate.

Tuesday, November 19 (Moon in Gemini) Imagination is highlighted. Watch for psychic events, synchronicities. Keep track of your dreams, including your daydreams. Ideas are ripe. You can tap deeply into the collective unconscious for inspiration. Universal knowledge, eternal truths, deep spirituality are the themes of the day.

Wednesday, November 20 (Moon into Cancer, 6:24 a.m.) Promote new ideas now; follow your curiosity. Freedom of thought and action is key. Think outside the box. Take risks; experiment. Variety is the spice of life.

Thursday, November 21 (Moon in Cancer)   The moon is on your ascendant. The way you see yourself now is the way others see you. You're recharged for the remainder of the month, and this makes you more appealing to the public. You're physically vital, and relations with the opposite sex go well.

Friday, November 22 (Moon into Leo, 6:57 p.m.) It's a number 7 day. Secrets, intrigue, confidential information play a role. You investigate, analyze, or simply observe what's going on now. You quickly come to a conclusion and wonder why others don't see what you see. You detect deception and recognize insincerity with ease. Gather information, but don't make any absolute decisions until tomorrow.

Saturday, November 23 (Moon in Leo)   Expect emotional experiences related to money today. You equate your financial assets with emotional security now. Watch how you spend your money, and make sure you have your priorities correct. Money and material goods give you a sense of security now.

Sunday, November 24 (Moon in Leo)   You're at center stage today, Cancer. Drama is highlighted. You feel like flaunting and celebrating. Be wild, imaginative; be the person you always imagined you might be. Play with different personae.

Monday, November 25 (Moon into Virgo, 7:11 a.m.)
It's a number 1 day, and that means you're at the top
of your cycle. You get a fresh start, a new beginning.
You can take the lead now, and don't be afraid to turn
in a new direction. Stress originality in whatever
you're doing.

Tuesday, November 26 (Moon in Virgo) The
moon is in your third house today. It's a good day for
expressing yourself through writing. Take what you
know, and share it with others. As you go about your
daily life, look for ways to succeed in whatever you're
doing. Expect an invitation to a social event.

*Wednesday, November 27 (Moon into Libra, 5:00
p.m.)* Ease up on your routines. Your attitude determines everything today. Take time to relax, enjoy
yourself, recharge your batteries. You can influence
people now with your upbeat attitude. In romance
you're an ardent and loyal lover.

Thursday, November 28 (Moon in Libra) The
moon is in your fourth house today. Spend time with
your family and other loved ones. Stick close to home.
You're dealing with the foundations of who you are
and who you are becoming. It's a good day for meditation and dream recall. Happy Thanksgiving.

*Friday, November 29 (Moon into Scorpio, 11:04
p.m.)* It's a number 5 day. Change and variety are
highlighted now. Think freedom, no restrictions. Release old structures; get a new point of view. You're

versatile and changeable, but be careful not to spread out and diversify too much.

Saturday, November 30 (Moon in Scorpio)   The moon is in your fifth house today. Your emotions tend to overpower your intellect. You're emotionally in touch with your creative side now. Be yourself; be emotionally honest. In love there's greater emotional depth to a relationship. Try not to be overly possessive of loved ones.

DECEMBER 2013

Sunday, December 1 (Moon in Scorpio)   The moon is in your fifth house. Your emotions tend to overpower your intellect today. Be yourself; be emotionally honest. In love there's greater emotional depth to a relationship now. You're also emotionally in touch with your creative side.

Monday, December 2 (Moon into Sagittarius, 1:32 a.m.)   There's a new moon today in your sixth house. New opportunities come your way related to your daily work. A new doorway opens. Others rely on you now. You're the one they go to for help. It's a good day to take care of any health issues. There could be something new available for you related to a health matter.

Tuesday, December 3 (Moon in Sagittarius)   The moon is in your sixth house. You could be feeling somewhat emotionally repressed today. Help others where you can, but attend to your own concerns as well. Keep your resolutions about exercise. Pay particular attention to diet and nutrition.

Wednesday, December 4 (Moon into Capricorn, 1:51 a.m.)   Mercury moves into your sixth house today. You're methodical and thorough now; you like everything in order. You're thinking about your health and physical well-being, but it's not an emotional issue. It's a good time to make an appointment for a physical or discuss any concerns with your doctor. You communicate well and get your ideas across, especially when you're helping others.

Thursday, December 5 (Moon in Capricorn)   The moon is in your seventh house today. The focus turns to relationships, both personal and business. You communicate smoothly and get along well with others now. You can fit in just about anywhere. You comprehend the nuances of a situation.

Friday, December 6 (Moon into Aquarius, 1:55 a.m.) It's a number 1 day, and you're at the top of your cycle. Be independent and creative. Don't let others tell you what to do. Get out and meet new people, have new experiences, do something you've never done before. Express your opinions dynamically.

Saturday, December 7 (Moon in Aquarius)   Mars moves into your fourth house today. You're strongly focused on your home life. You can accomplish a lot now. Work on a home-repair project. Beautify your surroundings. Try not to be overly aggressive; avoid being a disruptive force.

Sunday, December 8 (Moon into Pisces, 3:35 a.m.)
It's a number 3 day. You come out of your shell now.
You communicate well. You're warm and receptive to
what others say. Spread your good news. Ease up on
routines. Your charm and wit are appreciated. Play
your hunches.

Monday, December 9 (Moon in Pisces) The
moon is in your ninth house today. You're a dreamer
and a thinker. You impart knowledge and guide others in their intellectual development. It's a good time
to plan a long journey, especially if you're feeling restless. You yearn for new experiences. A foreign destination or a foreign-born person plays a role.

Tuesday, December 10 (Moon into Aries, 8:06 a.m.)
It's a number 5 day. Change your perspective. Approach the day with an unconventional mindset. (Easier said than done!) Think outside the box. Variety is
the spice of life. Take risks; experiment. Get ready for
change.

Wednesday, December 11 (Moon in Aries) The
moon is in your tenth house today. Your life is more
public. You gain an elevation in prestige, related to
your profession or whatever you do. You're more responsive to the needs and moods of a group and the
public in general.

*Thursday, December 12 (Moon into Taurus, 3:41
p.m.)* Secrets, intrigue, confidential information
play a role today. You might feel best working on your

own. You investigate, analyze, or simply observe what's going on now. You quickly come to a conclusion and wonder why others don't see what you see. It's best to hold off on making any final decisions for a couple of days.

Friday, December 13 (Moon in Taurus)   The moon is in your eleventh house today. You get along especially well with friends and members of a group. You work for the common good, but keep an eye on your own wishes and dreams. Your sense of security is tied to your relationships and friends.

Saturday, December 14 (Moon in Taurus)   Cultivate new ideas, but make sure that they're down-to-earth. It's a good day to use common sense and take a down-to-earth perspective on whatever you're doing. You're feeling sensual and opinionated today, but you also might tend to be somewhat stubborn if someone disagrees with you.

Sunday, December 15 (Moon into Gemini, 1:41 a.m.)   You're at the top of your cycle again. Be independent and creative. Don't let others tell you what to do. Get out and meet new people, have new experiences, do something you've never done before. Express your opinions dynamically.

Monday, December 16 (Moon in Gemini)   The moon is in your twelfth house today. After your busy Sunday, it's a good day to withdraw and work behind the scenes. You might communicate your deepest feelings to a friend, but otherwise keep your thoughts to yourself. Take time to reflect and meditate. Sort out all the chaos; put your plans together.

Tuesday, December 17 (Moon into Cancer, 1:17 p.m.)
With Uranus going direct in your tenth house today, you feel a strong need to work smoothly with fellow workers. Just make sure you receive the recognition that you deserve. There's also a full moon in your twelfth house, which suggests that you gain insight into a matter from the deep past. Take time to reflect and meditate.

Wednesday, December 18 (Moon in Cancer)   With the moon on your ascendant, you get your batteries recharged. You're physically vital, Cancer, and get along well with the opposite sex. You're also malleable and easily change your mind now. You're restless and uncertain what to do.

Thursday, December 19 (Moon in Cancer)   With the moon in your first house today, your thoughts and feelings are aligned. Others see you as you see yourself. You're feeling vital now. It's all about your health and your emotional self: how you feel and how you feel about yourself. You tend to search for ways to improve yourself.

Friday, December 20 (Moon into Leo, 1:48 a.m.)
You're creative and passionate today, impulsive and honest. Focus on making people happy today. Do a good deed for someone. Be sympathetic, kind, and

compassionate. However, avoid scattering your energies.

Saturday, December 21 (Moon in Leo) Venus goes retrograde in your seventh house today and stays that way until January 31. It's not a good time to get married or form a business partnership. You could have problems getting along and general disagreements. You also might have second thoughts later about any contracts you sign during this time.

Sunday, December 22 (Moon into Virgo, 2:20 p.m.) It's a number 8 day, your power day, Cancer. Speculate, take a chance. Focus on a power play. Open your mind to a new approach that could bring in big bucks. Be aware that fear of failure or fear that you won't measure up might attract exactly that experience. Unexpected money comes your way.

Monday, December 23 (Moon in Virgo) The moon is in your third house today. You're moving about in your everyday world handling chores. You're talking with close family, other relatives, and neighbors, getting your ideas across. You look to the past for inspiration. Try to control your emotions when dealing with siblings. Be particularly cautious if you're driving and talking on your cell phone.

Tuesday, December 24 (Moon in Virgo) Mercury moves into your seventh house today. You could find yourself serving as an arbitrator between two factions. You tend to deal with intelligent and articulate people now. A partnership plays a role. You get your ideas across.

Wednesday, December 25 (Moon into Libra, 1:18 a.m.)   Cooperation is key today. A partnership plays an important role in your day. That's been the case all week. Be kind and understanding. Family members play a role. Best not to make waves now; go with the flow. Merry Christmas!

Thursday, December 26 (Moon in Libra)   The moon is in your fourth house today. A love matter needs special attention. You're dealing with the foundations of who you are and who you are becoming. Best to stay home with your partner rather than go out with friends tonight. A parent plays a role. It's a good day for dream recall.

Friday, December 27 (Moon into Scorpio, 8:59 a.m.) It's a number 4 day. Tear down the old in order to rebuild. Be methodical and thorough. Your organizational skills are highlighted. Control your impulses to wander off task. You're building a creative base for your future.

Saturday, December 28 (Moon in Scorpio)   The moon is in your fifth house today. Be yourself; be emotionally honest. In love there's greater emotional depth to a relationship now. You're emotionally in touch with your creative side. It's a good day to take a chance, experiment.

Sunday, December 29 (Moon into Sagittarius, 12:38 p.m.)   It's a service day. Do a good deed for someone. Visit someone who is ill or in need of help. You're passionate but impatient. Be understanding, and avoid confrontations.

Monday, December 30 (Moon in Sagittarius)   The moon is in your sixth house today. It's another service day. Others come to you for help. You improve and refine what they started. Offer assistance, but don't deny your own needs. Take care of any health issues.

Tuesday, December 31 (Moon into Capricorn, 1:02 p.m.)   It's a number 8 day, a good day to buy a lotto ticket. It's your power day, your day to play it your way. You can go far with your plans and achieve financial success. Unexpected money comes your way.

HAPPY NEW YEAR!

SYDNEY OMARR

Born on August 5, 1926, in Philadelphia, Pennsylvania, **Sydney Omarr** was the only person ever given full-time duty in the U.S. Army as an astrologer. He is regarded as the most erudite astrologer of the twentieth century and the best known, through his syndicated column and his radio and television programs (he was Merv Griffin's "resident astrologer"). Omarr has been called the most "knowledgeable astrologer since Evangeline Adams." His forecasts of Nixon's downfall, the end of World War II in mid-August of 1945, the assassination of John F. Kennedy, Roosevelt's election to a fourth term and his death in office . . . these and many others are on the record and quoted enough to be considered "legendary."

ABOUT THE SERIES

This is one of a series of twelve *Sydney Omarr®
Day-by-Day Astrological Guides* for the signs of
2013. For questions and comments about the
book, go to www.sydneyomarr.blogspot.com.

COMING SOON

SYDNEY OMARR'S®
ASTROLOGICAL GUIDE
FOR YOU IN 2013

As we begin the new year, these expert forecasts for 2013 offer valuable insights about the past and extraordinary predictions for the future. Brimming with tantalizing projections, this amazing guide will give you advice on romantic commitment, career moves, travel, and finance. Along with year overviews and detailed month-by-month predictions for every sign, you'll learn everything that's new under the stars, including:

- What to expect from relationships with family and partners
- New career opportunities for success in the future
- Global shifts and world forecasts
- And much more!

Available wherever books are sold or at
penguin.com